# Confession
## of Happiness
### a Dark
### Account

# Confession of Happiness

## a Dark Account

## DIARY OF AN INTERNET AFFAIR

LISA TRAVIS

**To order additional copies of this book, contact:**
Xlibris Corporation
1-888-795-4274
www.Xlibris.com
Orders@Xlibris.com
39824

Thank you

To Ray, for all his creative assistance in making this account a reality, and for love and continuing emotional support.

# CHAPTER 1

Tell me what woman does not dream of the perfect man. Lots of women dream of handsome, romantic, obliging men that open doors and surprise us with a little something from time to time. Even surprise us with the rose bush to plant in the garden rather than a one time dozen roses in a vase. "There honey I've supplied you with a lifetime of roses," he says.

"Thank you sweetheart now you have no excuse from stopping to smell the roses with me."

Or perhaps one enjoys being surprised on your anniversary with a delightful candlelight dinner in that quaint little restaurant that is so unique. Oh! Or a picnic on the beach as the sun slowly melts in the west. What is your dream? What is your fantasy? You know that little thing in the back of your mind that urges exploding orgasms.

Let's take a little ride into the depths of a mind filled with explosive . . . creativity. Or shall we say a mind that searches for the perfect dashing male to sweep her off her feet and onto the saddle of a large white destrier. Or possibly that oversized 4x4 truck will do in a pinch.

Writing about oneself is never easy. It's not a strong forte of mine as well, so here goes. I have said many times before that 'I hate people'. It isn't so much an evasion from being in the presence of people. Listening to others has always been a strong point. Everyone has a story to tell, be it from mundane hardship of everyday living to elation of joyful events. The general populace is quite fascinating to say the least and as a people person I soak up knowledge from diverse values, customs, cultures . . . Deviating from contradictions already. I am one big contradiction struggling to make an honest stand here. Yes, the statement was previously made that I hate people but yet I am a good listener. Go figure! In all actuality it isn't dislike of everyone, better put it would seem that those in close proximity fail to provide support. Expectations of family and friends cannot seem to live up to my standards of what perfection should be.

Perhaps we should start from the beginning but only as a reference to the outcome. I was born the oldest in a struggling family wrapped around raising three kids. Our parents are highly creative, independent types with decent family values. They would have made wonderful hippies in the 60's but their time was too early for that. Mom's creativity is oil painting and my sister's is watercolor. They have an exceptional eye for details like color and hue and should pursue their craft with more gusto. With a sense of ambition as well as a good mentor mom could have made more of her gifted skill. Now dad is the master of science and math. He enjoys things, ideas and objects of an eccentric nature—proving that I get this broad Irish character quite honestly. Studying the Great Pyramid of Cheops and its mathematical equations to the physical plane of mankind was a fascination of ours in the 70's.

Growing up I was terribly shy, even to the point of being dreadfully backwards. That was in the 60's and 70's, a time that is clouded over from politics and cultural growth, deceit and starch reputation. You shift an inch one way and your reputation was shot all to hell. But you know here in the present progression of time changes in many ways while remaining the same in human nature. Starch stature of reputation remains supreme.

I had friends throughout junior high and high school. Oh we were goofy as most girls that age while making the best of situations through slumber parties and such. Each one of us would have benefited from good teachers, strong people with good hearts to direct us into worthwhile objectives like making good grades.

Please, take your kids under your wing. Raise their emotional awareness of this mad world around us while empowering them to reach their full potential. Teach them basic fundamentals of getting through this crazy thing called life. Listen to them, they have much to say! I have nieces and nephews, and there is one in particular, a godchild. We understand each other quite well as I try to help this youth through the difficult teenage years. Alas, this very smart and good kid takes after our eccentric Irish side of the family with a bull headed outlook very much like my own.

Ok, there is little need to discuss much about my youth. I lost my virginity at the age of 16. Enough said, let's leave skeletons in the closet. Nope. Not even rattle the old bones. Alright, maybe reference to a verbally abusive father yelling 'shut up' all the time is needed, pedophile uncle that jacked off while staring at me behind corners, and a first husband that only married me so that his mother would not kill herself. Ah gee. It's a wonder I don't hate men. I don't hate them.

Sadly issue of the pedophile uncle was brought to my parent's attention after he tried playing footsy with me under the holiday dinner table. Finally at the age of 18 I took mom and dad aside and explained instances stemming from the age of 12 when uncle showed up nude in my face as I tried to sleep. He claimed that the window behind me was broken. And then there was the time he made me hold his exposed privates while taking a ride on the motorcycle. Mom and dad both stated to the revelation that we can't let auntie know so let's just not say anything. Isolation and abandonment never felt so cold. My parents failed to support my grief and the pedophile uncle did not even receive reprimand behind a closed door from my overprotective father. To this day mom says she is very sorry. Dad does not recall instances or else changes the subject to the latest and greatest woodworking project of African snake wood. One must notice the subtle yellow streaks amidst the gentle range of red and brown hues, or was it green?

Does blindness soothe over deep pain of family living? How can something so familiar seem like such a stranger, unapproachable and unattainable? Obviously the lack of attention plays havoc to developmental issues of trust.

The uncle did have two other instances where children came forward professing that he did inappropriate things, like the garden hose that was not a garden hose and touching inappropriately, but somehow adults always pacified accusations. Are children to be seen and not heard? Were adults 30 years ago more passive than they are now? It was a different time but that is absolutely no excuse for skipping out on a much needed warning.

Ironically, concerning men, there is a particular instance as a teenager. The famous singing duo Hall and Oats had a popular song on the charts entitled 'Man eater'. I gallivanted through the house one day singing 'She's a man hater'. Dad heard the resonate line sung and quickly vocalized a loud reprimand that bellowed through the long halls. It seems quite funny now to recall. But I digress.

Let's get back on track . . . today I am married to a good hearted man, well liked by his peers, a physically strong but gentle natured man with good common working sense in most instances. Or as mom's best friend once stated 'one nice hunk of a man'. Talk about man crazy. Aw, but she is a sweet and romantic woman. I hear she's also seen Phantom of the Opera over thirty times. She's *in love* with the phantom.

To this day we have a good home with things in life that make existence pleasant and enjoyable. We dated for five years before marrying in our early 30's. Long enough to get to know someone you might say. He was fortunate to have lived at home until the age of 30. Maybe long enough to become a mama's boy but that's not always a bad thing. He also worked the same construction job that he had stepped into at the age of 16. Seems like a good start for a stable man and a stable relationship. Looks can be deceiving. One never knows what evils lurk behind closed doors.

When we first met I had been quite thankful to have found a stable individual after my bumpy start in life. During the first few years it seemed like here is a real guy, tender, sweet and giving of his heart. Throughout weekends together we talked constantly, communication flowed easily as we discussed everything. He taught me new customs that pertained to his world, taught me a new drive to succeed, philosophical thoughts I would like to emulate and create change with. Isn't it wonderful when you meet someone new and learn fresh qualities of living? Isn't that what draws people together? We see qualities in others that we are drawn to, tactics we wish to copy, attitudes that can make us a better person. That seems to be the basic magic of compatible togetherness. Mix that with genuine love and then tack on grandchildren and great grandchildren. Certainly anyone can visualize a marvelous 50th wedding anniversary they have attended.

For two decades I worked full time in the field of printing but no longer. I cannot bring myself to return to that crazy and demeaning life of misguided bosses. The subjective life burned my mental state one too many times along with my inability to fit into this local society. There will be more reference to the awful job fiasco later.

We have no children by choice which makes us a little spoiled and we enjoy traveling occasionally. I have seen and enjoyed many things in this lifetime and feel blessed. As was said before I enjoy studying diversified cultures and learning about this vast life and history of mankind. Perhaps to simply ask the philosophical question—what makes us tick? The thought has crossed my mind to study evolution of language from the beginning of hieroglyphics and cryptology into Greek, Latin and then advancement into Middle Ages . . . or to read H.G. Wells "The Outline of History" but, nah, as a fiery Leo that prefers instantaneous results that would take too much time.

Thanks to those Irish ancestors I am now proving how eccentric I can be. (Shush, a little Irish blarney doesn't hurt anyone.) So in returning this lofty imagination back to street level one might see that this tight little religious community of unimaginative thinkers bores me *tremendously*! This family that I married into, bless their hearts are a nice bunch (religiously known as the gentle people) but if I have to listen to Aunt Hattie's gall bladder transplant, or the cooing over precious little whoever's whatever, or the 24/7—twelve months out of a year arguments over the local basketball teams I'm going to go stark raving mad I tell you!

I have offended a few family oriented readers now. Sorry, but I was born without a single mothering gene in this core of flesh and bones. The blunt question was posed to my own mother at the age of 18 'can I get my tubes tied because I never want to have any kids'. She replied 'no, you may change your mind at a later date and besides having one might be good for you'. Yeah right mom. You are the one that yelled through the halls back in the 70's that you never wanted to have any kids. All you wanted to do was move to Carmel, California and explorer the idea of becoming a hippy artist. Look at me now and remember . . . you met my boyfriend as well that fateful Fourth of July. (A save must quickly be inserted here. My mother and I are actually very close and she has read these first few pages. The reader asks about her reaction? Laughter was the reaction that she gave. An auntie remarks that my mother is the kindest person she's ever known, which is true as well as my gentle maternal grandmother.)

On top of all this family chaos one night alone in my teenage room I said a prayer to God. "Please God do not let me have any kids and I will try to be nice to people in this lifetime." It seems we are keeping up our ends of the bargain. Knock on wood.

All this surface living is fine and dandy but—there is a dark side to all matters. A deep and delving place where the timid fear to go while cowering behind, forgive me, but religion for one. Also cowering behind the proprieties of everyday living. Are we not but the human animal? In all properness from being the intelligent mammal we are subject to gentle formalities of the day. So yes, discussion of sex in public is taboo to most, but then again those reading this account are not frightened by taboo.

Taboo, fear, and proprieties all set aside now. Let us continue unhindered by labels. Addiction . . . addiction to sex . . . porn . . . cheating on a spouse . . . swingers club . . . if your heart fails now. Close the book. Believe me this will progressively get worse.

Follow me and watch your step please as stagnant lichen only causes the rough hewn stepping stones to become slippery. Descending into the cave of obsession ability to see only grows deeper and darker while sound of the outside world is gradually absorbed by thick walls. As we notice a dramatic temperature drop I will claim viewing and delving into a realm that frightens some people away but there are a few persons that will peek. Furthermore you know who you are while peeking into a sexual nether world. Do we label this as wrong? Perhaps it's just another way of life. Perhaps my Lutheran upbringing nudges me to straighten my ways and come out of this cave of blindness. Nudge all you want! I have found happiness and joy in my way of life and through unconventional friends.

These circumstances did not happen overnight although some came into view quite early on. The most obvious being my husband's addiction to porn, normal for some guys who find that suggestive magazines are just a staple to living. In our world sexy magazines are mostly accepted. Just don't let them land in the hands of youth. Triple x-rated movies are also a norm that silently slip into DVD's late at night in some households. No one gets hurt. Of course we are unaware of the actor's personal lives. One can only hope that the actors are all 18 years of age among a few other evils which one dares not imagine, evils such as bondage, rape and murder. Underground tapes are still made which authorities need to catch the perpetrators and prosecute them to the extent of the law. Possibly an eye for eye would be appropriate in some instances. However in this day and age who are we to dictate to our peers or leaders what we deem as important, appropriate or fair?

And then there are strip clubs which my husband enjoys frequenting—most every Saturday night while I stay home alone. There are times when he has been to strip clubs both Friday and Saturday nights while I stayed home to entertain myself. Do I care? No. Does it affect me? Yes. Of course it does. It affects my self esteem as a woman. It affects my ability to be in the same room with him while nude for fear that he will judge my body as something less. How can I compete with young women in their twenties with tight young bodies and a flirtation he prefers over mine? Fine! If he prefers the company of young women every Saturday night then I will find someone that enjoys my company. What's good for the goose is good for the gander and this woman will certainly not be denied what is due to her.

I blame myself. I know. I know. You say don't blame yourself since he suffers from the addiction. But I will assume tormented blame. In my 30's I worked full time and came home tired and grumpy most evenings, just too tired for sex or even the simple act of bonding. Sound familiar? It's a common scenario for a high percentage of working couples in this world, has been and always will be. So it is my fault that I pushed him away. But you know what? The strange thing is he did not begin gallivanting to strip clubs on a regular basis until I stopped working. It was after I began staying home on a regular basis that he began going out alone most weekends—even before we acquired this computer. So although I blame myself for pushing him away sexually, I blame him for neglecting his wife and giving me this wonderful opportunity to advance my friendships with the opposite sex.

Strip clubs can be interesting though. I attempted to share the thrill with my husband a few times. In fact our outings aroused a little bi-curious nature. Some girls are very cute and very soft, and fun loving. I enjoy tucking dollar bills in the side of their thong or between their breasts as well as receiving lap dances, kissing those beautiful lips and caressing, hugging while pressing against those fleshy curves.

There was one particular night. She was a fairly attractive blonde and close to my age. The woman must have been in her mid thirties while me in my forties but not looking the age. (Good jeans, oops I mean good family genes. Oh, a high quality pair of jeans doesn't hurt either.)

The strip club was booming and crowded that evening. We had been conversing with an older man that happened to know someone that I used to work with. To my husband's far side was a group of college guys and to the front were two young couples seated at the ledge of the raised dance floor. Their wives or girlfriends had been to strip clubs before and knew what to expect. Not me.

The dancer sashshayed across the stage to the strong beat of loud music while wearing only a thong and extremely tall platform shoes. Stopping before them she then squatted down to their level.

It was the female customers that tipped by way of lifting their tops. I could not see completely or quite realized what was going on. The dancer hugged them, kissed their cheek and took the bills.

Toward the end of this particular dancers set my husband approached the stage to tuck her as well. She whispered in his ear, no big deal to me as it's his thrill, but then she looked in my direction and said, "I'm going to see what you've got before this evening is through." Meaning she was going to see my chest. Hubby laughed and told her they were nice. I just smiled and thought 'yeah right' if she thinks she is going to see my breasts.

Time went on and the blonde dancer returned to the stage for her next set. I had this feisty feeling that I sometimes get, similar to a dare or challenge which was also compounded by a couple of amarettos with seven-up. I said nothing and let it fester.

Watching and waiting for her to come around to our part of the stage I grabbed a dollar bill from hubby's front shirt pocket. He smiled and asked while knowing full well that I was going to tip the gal. I untucked my shirt and went to the edge of the stage. She saw me and came around with a large smile. Possibly it was a reflection of my own grin. I failed to know what to do and stood there like a dummy, but instantly her hand took the bill and boldly lifted my shirt and bra . . . and then you should've heard the room cheer! Man what a rush! The room cheered from girl on girl action. Isn't that a fantasy from a large percentage of men? As well as the threesome fantasy?

Quickly she put the bill in my cleavage and hugged me. Wow, bare breast to bare breast we were pressed together in a hug with a crowd gone wild. She was so soft and a subtle fragrance enveloped her, so sweet. I liked it. I also liked the reaction of the crowd. And you know what? Those two other girls didn't even get a peep from the crowd when they lifted their shirts.

Oh hubby was proud. When I returned to my chair it was hubby that was sitting next to the girl that had received the cheers. But in time the guy next to us continued conversation or possibly flirtation as hubby imagined, so it was time to move on. We said goodbye to the blonde girl and she hugged me again. I wish that we could have stayed to eventually get a lap dance from her. Who knows what else we could have accomplished in the back room. Possibly even sexual exploration or maybe even a meeting later that night.

I never did see that girl again. Nor has hubby. Darn. But I have been back to that particular establishment and have lifted my shirt and bra a few more times . . . but no, no more cheers from the crowd although a couple of small reactions. *Smiling here*

We went to the next club that same evening. Morgan, Devin and Diamond were their stripper names. Wow, if I had a daughter I would want her to resemble one of those three girls—beautiful sleek, slender girls with long tresses. They were 19 through 22 years old at the time and each spent five days a week in the gym. Their well toned bodies shown for all the hard work along with deep tans from tanning beds. That was it! That's all it took for me. I had to start working out, and working out I did.

It's been over two years now and I am still in better shape than ever. But along with feeling better and looking better comes a . . . an air about ones self. May I say that guys tend to glance more often? I've lost weight, my hair is longer and choice of clothing is different, perhaps more provocative would be the correct description. And I like it. So does hubby. Life is what one makes of it. Although I'm simple and an ordinary gal I fantasize about a little sports car, putting on attractive designer sunglasses and watching the guys stare. Anyone can have this air. It comes from within. It comes from the heart. Arrogance? No, it's called confidence. P.S. Confidence in the hands of an older woman that knows what to do with it is called—fun. And to my peers, sisters and counter parts . . . you go awesome girls!

That winter when I attended strip clubs with my husband several more things began to take place in our lives, including one particular evening when I looked fairly put together with hair and make up complete. I walked up to the doorway of his bathroom while wearing only a black satin panty and stated confidently with hands under my curves, "You may see some sexy boobs tonight but not all will be as nice as these." He glanced, smiled and then turned away as I stood there.

He turned back toward me, "What?"

"You're hopeless."

"What? I'm busy shaving," was all that he said.

I told this scenario to several people, mostly guys along with one girl, the guys all replied that they would have taken advantage of the situation. The girl remarked that her husband would have given some sort of feedback. Would most guys give a better or hands on reaction? I think so. What was I expecting? I don't know. I don't even care anymore. Hubby failed me and I'll not forget it.

Briefly to mention one other time I had approached while asking for a hug in the kitchen. He said, "No, I'll just leave you wanting a hug." I don't get it. What's going on here? Can anyone answer this question?

In summation of our strip club experience its left me with a certain self doubt, confusion in reference to my husband's reaction to our needs. There are two different things going on here: My inability (believe me as I have tried both physically and verbally) to attract my husband's attention in the exciting way that young strippers can excite him. Men enjoy looking at women and enjoy attention from a sexy young girl. I know this. Obviously this is the porn addiction taking over for my husband. Granted it's also just human nature of the male species in most instances. I will give that leeway to anyone countering my theory.

And number two is another factor we have not touched off on yet. My husband is afraid of me. Someone has stated that he is afraid of our intimacy. True. It's a shame that he can give his exciting sense of sexuality to strippers while leaving my self esteem wounded at the door starving for attention. But he is also afraid of me at times. As a bull headed Taurus he is quite capable of addressing his own thoughts and standing firmly upon hard terre cotta whereas I am a fiery Leo. One can see that I am highly independent, but out of the blue he sometimes is nervous that I am going to growl or bite his head off over a mishap that's taken place.

Alright, I know the meaning of this fear. It is confusion under heated circumstances weighted with assumption of guilt over the action. When I get mad he assumes responsibility for the mishap when the case is only my frustration at the moment. Example: spilled milk—he is afraid that I will bite his head off for spilling it. I am only mad that the mess needs to be cleaned up. The anger is not aimed at him.

Many women can confer with this instance. God bless these poor guys that have to put up with spirited women. Perhaps we need more marriage counselors available to iron out our pitiful differences. Cost affordable, mind you, perhaps even $25-$50 seminars. Any professional takers? Remember men do not appreciate counseling for the most part. They can't sit still long enough to talk about their feelings much less anyone else's. So a quick seminar might just do the trick, fast, efficient, direct and to the point. Shock effect is a valuable tool. Anything to begin thrusting open the doors of communication.

And to the self imposed therapists I hear you as well. So I am probably sending out faint signals to my husband? If signals that subtle can affect ones life then what does it mean for him to leave me at home every Saturday night while he gallivants to strip clubs? Huh?

So . . . how did this all start? How did this strong independence and confidence in nature begin on my part? As was stated before I worked full time for many years. The work was enjoyable while co-workers were an outlet for friendship and conversation, but bosses were most always a pain in the butt. One boss went to prison for money laundering. Another one ripped my phone from the wall and cleared my desk by a sweep of his hand as he was unhappy with the phone conversation. Co-workers agreed that the bi-polar part-time minister needed to be taken out and physically shot. Also in my working experience two other bosses were total bitches, etc. We won't even mention the drug runners at the trucking company as that is a complete and other novel in itself.

Once my last employment closed its doors I told someone that I would completely lose my mind. The breakdown came close, dangerously close as information was revealed to this individual which tree in our side yard that my demise would be accomplished behind. The tree is now gone due to rotting and a fire as is the need for demise, but thought of the end had been severe. For three months I wallowed in deep self pity. Hit the walls as well as a wooden kitchen cabinet with my fist several times (an Irish auburn temper ye know). No broken bones though. Thank you for asking. But I definitely saw stars with the temper. My head ached severely while fearful that a stroke was imminent and I screamed at the cabinet after pounding upon the wood, "Bring it on! Bring it on!"

And then remarkably one day not very long after that episode a pleasant thought hit me in return most likely by divine intervention. It was a thought of the Middle Ages . . . of England . . . of a castle. In my youth I had created a scenario over and over again in my head and now in this middle aged status I needed to write it down.

The fuzzy image was of a cold stone castle turret and the curving staircase that ascended to the right. To the right because in sword fight a man is usually right handed. (What happens if the man is left handed? Good question.) Anyway the warrior needs to balance his sword in the midst of battle. However in my scenario there is no battle at this moment in time. There are two shadowy figures engulfed in semi-darkness of the turret . . . figures of a young man and young lady. They are fleeing, fleeing up the stairs in a rush of adrenalin. He pulls at her hand as they dash through the cold stone monstrosity. Golden curls of the young lady's waist length tresses bounce with movement while fabric of her gown flounces, and the train gently glides over each stone riser. You ask where they are going. To a place where England's great King Edward III secretly entertained important Cardinals and dignitaries two generations earlier, to a secret chamber where the lady in waiting and the king's guard would create the first earl in the knight's lineage.

And write I did! With notebook and sharpened pencil in hand I wrote most every day, on average eight pages a day. It was a beautiful story of a knight and damsel in distress, romantic, heart wrenching. It followed the lines of a famous battle between England and France and my knight fought gallantly against miserable odds. He won the damsel back into his arms two seasons after the war. Along with their unruly illegitimate son who grew up to be an honorable knight as well.

The novel was finished in three months. Research had been a mental blast as endorphins bloomed through every marvelous, colorful detail. And what made it easier was this great computer that I had begged for, for Christmas that year.

The following spring I wrote another novel. The story of a legal secretary that finds romance in Louisiana with a contractor and again the book was finished in three months. My writing was simply *awful* but I enjoyed every moment of their wonderful creation.

Research of this second novel came after the fact when we vacationed in New Orleans. I feel blessed to have seen the wonderful city before the terrible hurricane and would love to go back and tour places of interest that was missed the first time around. Also experience beignets and coffee for breakfast in a quaint little café which my husband refused to do.

Oh, and I might also mention that hubby found the strip clubs on Bourbon Street which he patronized three nights out of our vacation while I stayed in the room alone for two evenings. Yup, how sad is that? At least I had a friend (Ray) to call on two of those nights. This friend appreciated my company and wished that he was the man beside me in that large antique room as I wished for the same.

One of those nights I did go out with my husband, the first night. Yes, our vacation that I had planned so carefully in advance, a vacation that certainly could have been indulgent in a romantic kind of way. So one evening I did join him. Stepping into the last club that evening the dingy establishment was advertised as live sex acts with male and female. Well it wasn't. The average looking couples remained in their skimpy costumes. But one particular pair invited us for a lap dance. (Excuse me as temper is already beginning to flare.) My husband hands the woman a hundred dollar bill and asks for change before they begin the lap dance. They conned us out of $80.00 of the hundred. Excuse me again, but my husband can easily hand a stripper the better part of a 'c' note but cannot take me out to a quaint little café for beignets and coffee because it would cost too much! I rest my case. We are incapable of taking vacations together. No more. I also remind him of this episode from time to time as fantastic leverage in making a worthwhile point known.

Let's change the subject now to lower my blood pressure. In reality our minds are not always in the gutter. This spastic nonsensical mentality is set aside as day to day living is taken seriously along with chores and household duties. In the outside world we are perceived as a typical couple, nothing out of the ordinary to neighbors, friends and most family.

Reality of summer came along with serious outdoor work that needed to be accomplished. I enjoyed warm summer days taking care of my flower garden, planting and cultivating lush greenery while surrounded by colorful floribunda, the goldfish pond and an assortment of farm cats. They thoroughly enjoy my company and we sunbathed together lounging away many hot summer days. By August I was bored. Oh, and I forgot to mention the guilt—the guilt of no longer working and bringing in an added income, but I couldn't force the issue. The boss in prison, the one that needed to be shot, and the two bitches. Yes this all has something to do with the fact that I have trouble with authority figures. Blame that on my father and the pedophile uncle. Ok fine, blame it on my predisposition that I won't try. Grrr, I'm not going to try! I've had it up to yonder with trying. Please, hold Dr. Phil at bay. Dr. Phil would reduce me to a pitiful pile of blasted rubble in an instant. Perhaps this lingering guilt and inability is still prevalent within my tormented soul.

So by August 2003 boredom set in. I had a computer. I could easily get online. Hmm, a deep question began to formulate. What were these chat rooms that people were talking about? Most of the discussion seemed to be that it was a highly dangerous game but curiosity won over reserve and I made the required member nickname for a well known site. I tried live chatting late one Saturday night and oh my gosh! Sunday was a blooming daze. I felt physically violated. The men had typed such raunchy words and content across the screen. It was appalling! I was such an innocent individual, caring, naive and backward to a fault while this strange medium of communication seemed like such a nasty realm of sexual perversion.

My husband had made his trip to the strip clubs Saturday night and Sunday morning he relayed his evening of barely clad women and their provocative conversations. Sunday mornings are always for hearing gory details of lap dances, flirtatious conversations of sexual preferences or of just how hot the girls looked. Compliments are freely handed out by the girls over his clothing or fragrant cologne which he pours on quite thickly. They also remark favorably while running their fingers through his thick hair or across those broad shoulders. One can see why he eats up this continuous attention. At this juncture it might also be added that he has received private nude dances that included a hand job for him once. He has touched between the girl's legs, and yes, he has even given oral contact to girls in private rooms. Do I care? No. It's all so stupid to me. Let me take that back. There is one thing that affects me. He has remarked on more than one occasion that he enjoys looking at young female genitalia—tight, small and unstretched in their youth. That borders on sick. Forgive me, too much shockingly said.

This Sunday morning I held back and said nothing of the chat room experience although the out of my mind daze continued throughout the afternoon. I had to say something, and then carefully I approached him on the matter while explaining a strange evening on the computer. He was curious as we discussed the subject quite rationally. I explained about entering a British chat site and that the boys were obscene foul-mouthed little perverts. I also said that a 20 something guy wrote that he wanted to fuck me. In hindsight that was the last site that any beginner should enter. There are milder places suited for temperate women. Not that I frequent those either mind you.

My husband didn't say much to the experience that I had explained. He didn't ban me from doing it again or anything like that. Perhaps it's just his naivety to so many things in the outside world, especially computers of which he knows nothing of. Thank goodness he has not discovered the internet or his level of porn would careen off the charts while needing a strong dose of detox. Come to think about it now there's a striking idea for the medical community—detox for internet perverts.

With time curiosity won over reserve and I was drawn into chat rooms again, through the week now as well. Learning the hard way like most of us do I inquired about specific jargon and abbreviations that make up the nether world. Men continued to be perverted pigs wanting to perpetrate sexual acts. They want to get to know a woman or meet in person. No, no, no to anyone curious about this realm. It *is* a very dangerous game. The person can be lying, or they can be an undercover cop, or you can loose your life to a killer. Protect yourself and your children by never letting a stranger into your personal surroundings, no matter how charming you perceive that person to be. Think of it this way—a perverse person talking over your head in an unwelcome sexual manner is comparable to raping your mind.

Quickly I found a safer room to chat in. It was a bi-sexual room where men were not allowed and I would go in day after day. This was an interesting way of meeting people from all over the United States while discussing weather changes, daily family life, sharing jokes and laughter. Discussions were all innocent enough but unfortunately this specific site became 'pay to chat' so I moved on.

It was around Halloween when I discovered a fun room with lively people. Trying hard to fit in I actually seemed to be accepted at the time. This new medium was an outlet for making friends, something that I failed to have in real life. Being from a very small community and an outsider in a cliquish religious area I was a prisoner in my own home. Granted a home with everything I needed and my pets but still a secluded prisoner. I needed this outlet! I needed friends and people to talk to, to share with, to laugh and banter with as was previously granted while working full time. I was now receiving a healthy dose of it through this strange medium.

But being this feisty person deep inside I guess I didn't play the way they preferred. There was a certain guy that had engaged conversation with me on occasion. He was from out east and a diehard chatter. He knew the ropes and had spoken on the phone with some regular girls from the room. One evening the opportunity for us to talk on the phone presented itself. This was the first time that I had physically spoken with someone from the internet and he called my cell phone at around two in the morning. I was exhausted but we chatted for awhile. The conversation was interesting and flowed easily. We didn't have cyber sex or talk sexually. It was just an innocent dialog similar to two people conversing in a bar.

A couple weeks later the lively room was hopping and I jumped right in typing words across the scrolling screen. Our male friend was being ganged up on by the girls just the way he enjoyed it. I must have played a little too hard as the tone of the room suddenly changed. To this day I still don't believe I really did anything inappropriate as I only went to sit by one of the popular girls, the one that he was picking on. But suddenly it was me they were ganging up on now. One by one key people of the room began to place my nickname on ignore, the worst thing that could happen. I was being severely rejected for some trivial reason that was unexplained and it was not a good feeling. A sweet gentleman that was a regular noticed the scenario taking place and remarked with a positive comment but I left it alone while silently retreating from the room.

Of course it made me angry and thoughts of how to get even with those people ran predominately through my mind. Perhaps if a sexy stripper entered the room guys would take notice and be drawn to her. And that is what I did. Well, to make a long story short the opportunity to get even with that specific fellow never presented itself but guys were certainly interested in the stripper. And shame on me but the sexy lady even had a photo of a very pretty model. Alright, I sense a majority of readers lambasting me. I know it was wrong and we should not behave as others do. One only knows how many profile photos are phony and of course I would not want to be fooled either.

My sense of shame was slim at the time. These nicknames that were viewed day in and day out meant nothing to me. Sure they were close friends with one another and had enjoyed each others company for many years perhaps. They had talked on the phone and had truly become actual friends. I was a newcomer into their world. Simply a stranger and strangers are not to be trusted especially from the internet.

However on the other hand what does it really matter whether I had created this phony nickname or not? People are people and chat is simply chat. It's personality that matters in the long run and we are not really going to meet that person in real life. Now are we?

# Chapter 2

Communicating with others on the internet really opens up a new medium. We're connecting on a new level, a private secretive level where one can expose as much personality as you like. It's a socializing process not to be judged by your looks, your age or social standing in life. The cloak that we wear in everyday living cannot be seen by others when we are online and alone. Perhaps to begin with—its friendliness, how well we relate to one another by way of words typed on a flat screen. It is most definitely live chat, an instant reaction to a string of sentences while remaining in the comfort of our homes. Our guard is down while we sit in comfy clothes sipping coffee in the morning, sharing with friends, teasing each other, wishing one another a good day, lending an ear to one that is having a bad day, simply providing emotional support. Isn't that friendship? Isn't that what we all wish for? Sure and where is the harm?

Discussions bounce around rapidly from several diversified personalities talking all at once, male and female, young and older as well as from many different walks of life. Opinions are splattered in abundance across the infinite scrolling screen, some given freely while others ask questions on matters perceived as important to them. Possibly one just needs to be aware that answers will usually fall into the realm of sexuality by sassy types. It is the way of the web, otherwise known as adult humor.

However there are pigs in the morning as well. Sneaky guys slithering low along the fence line that would like to discuss explicit sex or sexual acts. They wish to get a live wire to share a scenario of copulation as they relieve their carnal urges while sitting at the computer. Dirty and nasty huh? There are different degrees of pigs and yes I have chatted enough that I know varied degrees. A horny guy is a horny guy begging and pleading to 'please stay. Do you like phone sex? I have 10 hard inches for you. I'm so horny can you help me out?' Good grief. Sounds like a personal problem demanding a personal conclusion. Can't they see that a computer is just a computer made for real tasks of importance? I'm sure they would state that their personal relief is a real task of importance as well.

Typing this now the whole thing seems so disgusting. To this day pigs are quickly ignored or if someone insists in giving a hard time . . . well, I sadistically enjoy shooting them down. Sorry, but I do enjoy messing with a nasty guy's mind long enough to let him realize he's got a viper ready to vehemently strike. Life is to be lived passionately and unfortunately fervent does not always mean tender and caring. They can take care of themselves and certainly can do it well. Enough said.

Under the stripper nickname I quickly became friends with a nice fellow. Perhaps I should also admit that this guy was my first internet boyfriend. We just seemed to click personality wise. He was suffering from a difficult time under the thumb of his strict father, although the guy was 30 years old at the time and still living at home with his parents. We engaged in conversation for hours on end. It quickly became a habit for both of us, our terrible addiction. (Another point to make about chatting is that it can become a time consuming habit, a strong one at that! So many people admit that it takes up quite a lot of their time. More than it should.) Also, it must be stated that I was not the first girl this guy had attached too. He is a diehard chatter, extremely polite on the surface while suffering sexual addictions of his own although he seemed so down to earth and genuine too.

We talked on the phone I believe that first night. Of course hubby was out to the strip clubs. To say the rest is history at this juncture would be a cop out. I still see (let's call him Ben) in the chat room but we no longer communicate on a constant basis. My choice. Possibly every six months or so we say 'hello' or 'how are you' but that's about it.

In the beginning Ben and I quickly fell hard for each other while talking on the phone several times a week. We even discussed meeting one day in Memphis, Tennessee at a well known strip club on a Saturday night. We laughed and communicated most everything in our secretive world although I was living a lie as the stripper at the time. Shame on me but let's call the sexy lady Sue. Ben was totally interested in Sue's life as an exotic dancer and wanted to come watch her work sometime. Reality was firmly in place though while knowing we would most likely never meet, but it was fun to fall into the realm of fantasy. We continued talking on the phone late at night while enjoying the benefit of intimate phone sex. It was exhilarating. Ben was awesome. He came so hard. The man is so sexy, something that I didn't have in my real life. I needed his attention! I finally had a boyfriend to fill the void!

Christmas was quickly approaching and Ben wanted to purchase a Christmas gift for Sue. I put my foot down while completely refusing the suggestion even though it seemed like a thrilling idea. Ben was sweet and insisted he wanted to go through with this gesture just as a friend. He took my address and went online to purchase the present while I went to the postmaster and added Sue's name to my address. Sue was my cousin that was going to stay with us over the holidays I told the postmaster. Yes I am slick, sly, I lie convincingly. Please, please keep Dr. Phil away! Heaven forgive me I have lied many times. I am only sorry in having to admit the truth but I had to undergo this experience, this transformation. I needed to live passionately. At least my boyfriend cared. Sigh.

For Christmas I received a beautiful little diamond necklace. Oh, I was on cloud nine. Life was beyond measure! It showed on my face, in my attitude, in my actual existence but we couldn't go on this way. It wasn't right. It wasn't fair in the long run as things rapidly became obvious that Ben was a player stringing me along and of course I was playing him too in this lie. Three weeks later Ben was informed that Sue was not my real name. He silently listened before calmly stating 'you're crazy'. The statement was thoroughly deserved. I deserved anything and everything that he threw at me as dishonest shoulders stiffened with the weight.

It was after we both cried on the phone one dreary winter afternoon when Ben and I broke up. It was a relief at the time to be free of the impropriety as the need to move on became obvious. But wouldn't you know it. We were back together within two or three weeks. This time heralding from the starting gate we began with the truth in our mini online affair again. Phone sex was still awesome and we each had an understanding friend to lean on. I also paid the sweet guy for the necklace which is still worn sometimes to this day. He is also happy to hear that I wear it too. All in all Ben and I lasted about two seasons but remained close friends for over a year.

Before paying for the little diamond necklace I told my husband all about fooling Ben and the fact that the guy was gutsy enough to send the Christmas present. My husband thought the deception was bad but I don't remember him going off on any strong tangent over the matter. In the long run my husband allows me the freedom to have online 'boyfriends'. However hubby was a bit jealous that Ben had purchased a better Christmas present than he did.

What Ben and I did is not an exception to the world of internet communication or internet dating if you will. There are many people out there on the net doing the exact same thing that we did. This world is not what it used to be since the formation of java script. There are liars, cheating spouses, sex addicts and perverts using the internet as a way to further their dark obsessions. We have all been witness to the continuing horror stories in the news. Sometimes I hear accounts on a monthly basis of another woman that is cheating on her husband by way of the internet. A portion of these nicknames that I view daily are actually meeting one another for sex. It is epidemic, it truly is. My gosh, these woman are even getting pregnant by strangers and then raising the child of a one night stand all alone! The stories that come from out there are not for the weak of heart or for old fashioned values. Many years ago old fashioned values were to be cherished but alas technology is changing our ways. I know morals and values still have to exist for the majority of the public though.

This same winter the second week of February arrived, almost Valentine's Day in 2004. My profile now portrayed the real me with an actual photo to boot. While chatting one day a whisper window popped up on the screen, a private place where two people can talk alone. Let's call him Steve. This man is still with me today in instant messenger, but barely due to our brutal antagonism, extremely brutal as you shall see unfolding.

At the time Steve was different. He was a little bit of a pig but never wished to cyber or engage in phone sex. His style of chat was quite unique compared to others as this persona quickly exposed heavy intellect along with a character quite sly. Politely I asked for his profession. The following statement was typed across the screen 'NYC attorney'.

I was completely fascinated! Wow! How could a little country girl be worthy of the presence from someone so high up the social and eco ladder? Steve spoke of a rich and beautiful life to which I fell hook line and sinker. It was a life of financial ease with a hired housekeeper, hired drivers, a personal trainer, steam room and weekly massages by a professional masseuse. There were gifts to his women of expensive perfume, cashmere, flowers, jewelry and fine lingerie from La Perla. What woman wouldn't be attracted by this excess of finery? Of course he could have been lying the whole time but to this day I still believe he is basically truthful. Even if he is truthful should he be considered rude for bragging and drawing women into his lair by professing excessive wealth under a veil of intrigue? He should stand accused of the crime. Maybe it is partly me. He came along at a time in my life when I was seriously searching for the perfect man to fill some sort of romantic role in my existence.

We did not communicate every day but I absorbed his words like crazy. Secretly I was jealous of his way of life. I could only dream of power and prestige, and of a man's complete love for a woman in the way that Steve described it. He never knew this but he made me cry so many times. I cried for what I could not have, for a Midwestern life that is so deficient on many levels, for a husband that would never be the man that Steve portrayed. Excuse me as I dry my eyes. My God it's been years since we first chatted and he still has this compelling affect on me! Alright, for the sake of a good therapist Steve has only given me the description of a life and lifestyle. I have not been privy to his image in photo or otherwise so one can only imagine the physical presence of this man by his mere description from words. Steve could be and is most likely an ordinary guy that plays women . . . and a dickhead that pisses me off too.

Where's the girl with the sports car and designer sunglasses that rides around high on confidence while teasing the boys? She's out to lunch. Sorry but she is only capable of teasing local boys that will whip their head around for an ordinary girl.

On a weekly or bi-weekly basis we quietly opened the doors to this secret world in our instant messengers. Steve and I shared sexy scenarios and situations of men and women. Elaborate scenarios of flirtation similar to nude sunbathing at a boat club, or on the town while I wore a little black dress. I have never owned the desirable little black dress in my life and most likely will never wear one. He asked 'what would you do should a stranger approach from behind and whisper in your ear?' Well if it were Steve *smiling here* . . . What if you were sitting in a restaurant and the man quietly stated 'slip off your panties and put them in your purse'. Sorry buddy but that's not me. With my luck we would get caught in an embarrassing situation.

We rarely put ourselves in the equation of sexuality because we're only exchanging ideas as strangers. His fascination is not equal to mine since he only enjoys killing time while working from the office.

Over the expanse of several days Steve continually asked for pictures, a quest that is his addiction. A friend had loaned us their digital camera the previous fall and there were tasteful photos of me taken from around the house stored in the computer. These photos were shown to Steve but he requested sexy ones. I said no. But of course with curiosity I wanted to try proving that it could be done. The family friend loaned us the digital camera again and I wrestled with the frustrating device to no avail. I couldn't ask for help from nervous fear should they should ask what I was doing.

Valentine's Day weekend hubby was away from home while attending a stockcar race down south and Steve had been given this knowledge earlier in the week. I went online late Saturday afternoon and met Steve in messenger. This was unusual because he is *never* online on a Saturday or Sunday. I fumbled with the digital camera in a series of comical events. It failed to work or perhaps more like the operator failed to make it work and little was accomplished. However I thanked Steve for meeting with me on Valentine's Day, a deed that I never forgot although his intent was not so honorable while wishing to receive risqué photos.

The following day I begged for my sister the photographer to come over. Film was loaded into the regular camera and we took tasteful boudoir photos of me in sexy nightie attire. Laughing the whole time we had fun with lighting and posing and of course I stated that the pictures were for my husband for Valentine's Day, but they were actually for Steve. A week later the photos arrived in individual prints and on CD disk to download onto the computer. The photo prints were hidden for the time being as the CD was quickly downloaded.

To make a long story short, Steve replied 'not bad' to the photos. He always says 'not bad' to things. Among sternly replying 'no' when he means don't waste my time on other matters. He comes across the wire as being such a hard ass. And yes, my husband received his sexy boudoir photos. Oh, he looked them over quite quickly and was a bit surprised that we accomplished such an off the wall project, but into the drawer the photos went never to be accessed again. Well, not until I accessed them for someone else (Ray) at a later date.

One night in April I had a strange dream full of words jumbled in a unique prose. Sometimes I avoid these thoughts and go back to sleep but this one was so unique that I jumped out of bed and began writing. The scribbling was then studied in the morning. A unique pattern was there. It made sense but was not complete. So the next night more of the unique prose came to me. Again I jumped out of bed and wrote the next few lines. By morning I put the two ramblings together and typed this poem on the computer. Now grant you poetry is not my thing but this needed to be created.

## The Thinker

Once upon a time in a land far away
Lived a lawyer of great intellect and strength.
On a day of lack luster he suddenly stepped
Out into the world of another.
Carelessly he stepped by strokes of the key
Into the den of the Lioness.

The Lioness quite wise and able herself
Held wisdom with knowledge of ages.
Sly and quite cunning; compare that to the fox,
A deep thinker thus containing her own very well.

The girl quite cute not superficial to boot
A student of Socrates and Plato
Studied Ideal of Man, but it failed to pan
Or get her any closer to men.

One day he asked for an explicit story to be told
Of which her short answer was "no"
Her pen set down gently to the side of the desk
As though returning the scabbard with sword.

Contemplation was quiet, knowing not which way to turn.
Times ticking relayed to the other.
A diapason of sound would have rang all round,
But to that timbre there was not even a tone.

Blind sided by his charm she wanted but more
But alas could not find the reward.
The reward so you see is what was wanted but gee,
The reward from a screen is just flat.

Although should reward come from mere words
Of this one's held thought all along.
Because of mere words that form image of mind
They mold the vast thoughts of another.

But of words I have many all jumbled and construed.
Locked up in books all abound.
So reward I surmise comes in all shapes and size.
I suppose desire of reward is just greed.

One afternoon I gave Steve his present of this poem. He quickly offered one correction of which I made by adding an 's' to shapes. He then simply remarked 'cute'. I took that as a good thing and smiled quite pleased with his reaction.

But then he inquired, "So what would be reward?"

"The sound of your voice or a photo."

"Nope."

Oh well. The present was only a gift. I did not need a reward although I would have appreciated a small gesture larger than 'cute'.

During progression of a grey winter while shivering from cold, dreary days Steve and I discussed vacations. Hubby had just returned from his Florida trip with the guys so it seemed like it would only be fitting that his wife should have an escape too. Many things crossed my dreamy mind. We had been to Hawaii. Mexico would be lovely to see again, someplace warm and tropical. Isn't that what people fantasize about during this frozen time of year? Steve commented that I should just treat myself to a vacation alone. The uncertain idea was remarkably intriguing, about as intriguing as Steve is to my psyche.

In time Expedia was discovered as I played with the idea of traveling alone. I could do it! I could prove my independence to everyone that doubted my abilities. I am still a viable person able to accomplish things in this lifetime. Besides I have a sister-in-law that sees me as less than a woman because I no longer hold down a full time job. I would prove to her to back off and stop the incessant jealousy laced with catty comments. This meek and mild woman has been jealous of me from day one as I worked outside the home full time. The poor woman is also tied at the overly fleshy hip to her husband and with serious problems to boot. I see her viability as deficient, unable to go out into the world alone as I had accomplished in the past. Her small soft hands are no match to mine which fit nicely into a pair of boxing gloves.

And I did it! Hubby agreed to let me travel alone. We carefully checked over different hotel packages that were offered through the site. He allowed financing of the trip from our savings as I chose a resort in the Bahamas and ordered it with a king sized bed, four nights and five days, Monday through Friday. I was proud of myself and thanked Steve for the exciting idea. And also invited him to come along of which he quickly and gracefully declined. Whatever. My vacation was going to happen whether Steve joined me or not.

Oh, and you ask why didn't hubby go with me? Several reasons. We had taken a honeymoon cruise to the Bahamas and he didn't want to revisit the area. His work prevailed while construction boomed in May when the weather warmed. And someone had to stay home to take care of our livestock. It's always been difficult for us to find a babysitter that can care for the animal menagerie as well as the potted plants. Maybe it's a little bit of perfectionism to continually maintain everything in its particular place. You know details matter whether they are legitimate or otherwise.

Late March the chat room was on the computer screen early in the afternoon. Not much was going on at the time. I was becoming an old pro at this and chose cantankerous battles carefully however it slowly became boring on this particular day. The strong addiction was still there but I was about ready to move on to something more realistic like housework or exercising when a private message window opened.

"Hi."

"Hello."

"How are you?"

"Wonderful and you?"

"Good. Are you married?"

"Yep, you?" I asked.

"Yes." Brad answered before asking, "Horny?"

Well the conversation didn't quite go this way word for word but it's pretty close to the majority of whispers.

To give Brad an answer I stated, "No, I was just about to leave but I could stay and talk for a bit."

"I'd like that and we don't have to cyber."

Brad was strongly attracted by the stripper's nickname and continues to make reference to it to this day. Sorry, but revelation of the nickname could be traced back to our identity by some and I will protect Brad at all costs. Brad and I chatted for hours some afternoons although he was playing on the computer from work. He is an executive in California with an honorable career in software engineering. His strong intellect and gentle nature shown instantly similar to Steve's with no nonsense as well as direct with a hint of caring underneath, but Brad was not Steve. Brad was married. I received his photo and wow. The man was good looking, tall with slender build, a very nice smile, blonde hair and beautiful blue eyes. Mmm, my surfer dude.

In the beginning we revealed a little about ourselves, our lives. Of course it held a basic underlying flirtation. Brad is very flirtatious. He is extremely good at this and sensual as well. If I have learned anything about my sexuality it is that I am also very sensual. Steve would attest to the fact too since he first pointed out this trait. Life is to be lived passionately and sensually with the tender caress of a man and woman while enmeshed within the bond of physical passion, two naked bodies pressed together, their fire and electric current boiling to the point of culmination . . . of merging, of watching one another's eyes has he enters her with their exploding rush of pleasure.

My Lover seduced me. He seduced me with great finesse. Each time we were together in instant messenger he made my heart flutter from erotic imagination. That is until I learned to seduce him in return, our time together only proceeded to achieve better and better highs. Years later we still remark that we have never experienced anything like this before. Our emotional affair is awesome—this bond that we share and phone sex in the evenings from his office. We have made waves while I enjoy the privacy of bath time or else he tucks me into the sheets when I am alone. Love making is so much better when we are completely alone.

Brad has the sexiest voice which I enjoy very much and he has remarked the same of me. During our time together we exploded passionately many times, in the beginning maybe once a month on an average. But you know in reality, he has stated and I am in full agreement on this point. We probably would not have this bond if we were to meet in real life. Reality is not the same as erotic imagination. We bounce off one another's words. He is an aficionado of words as well as fine wine. We create scenarios, dreams and fantasies. Oh they have been good. Of course I cannot tell you any of these stories since they belong to us in our private world. I would never kiss and tell. *Wink*

Never before have I known provocation to be as evocative as this . . . as this passion for Brad. Whew.

And so Brad and I began chatting before the Bahamas vacation. Steve wasn't going with me so I asked Brad to come along. 'No' he replied. As much as he wished for the fantasy he was unable to join me. But . . . he would be able to call the hotel late in the evenings.

Monday, Tuesday and Thursday nights he called. Brad felt an unbelievable rush of tantalizing excitement as he dialed the hotel late in the day and asked for my specific hotel room. The enthusiasm in his voice makes me smile. It's a breathy sound expelled from turned up corners of a mouth engulfed in a grin.

The first night I was woken up at 9:30 pm. I had been awake since 2:30 am that Monday morning to catch the flight but that didn't stop us. We were wired from adrenalin and a strong sense of arousal from our secretive world. Quietly he slipped into bed, between the sheets with me. The phone sex was awesome. With Brad it's always awesome . . . and real. With a strong sense of stimulation we can actually feel one another's presence, caressing arms, roaming hands, lips, heat, fire, passion, his manhood, my curves. Blood pumping through our veins, riding the edge while holding the top of the wave and then suddenly the bottom drops out with a loud vocalization of release. One explodes first and then the other. Afterward I lay in his comfortable arms as he floats in nirvana, resting my head on his broad chest, listening as the strong heartbeat slowly subsides. His fingers leisurely glide through my tresses while we strongly contemplate another round of indulgence. Fantasies are almost more erotic than the real thing at times. Arousal comes from stimulation of the mind and with a powerful partner the mind can go far.

Otherwise I behaved myself with a good book on the vacation and sunned on the beach each day. What a great tan I received that week. In the evenings I took walks along the beach, along the boulevard or to a sandwich shop a mile and a half up the street. And no, I wasn't hit on by any flirtatious guy or approached with any unwanted attention. Confidence of ego was mostly in place but something else just wasn't quite right. The excess body weight was off but the look of housewife or older woman was still there so it seemed.

The trip had been completely invigorating, embolden to the senses which only set the stage toward future events. I had accomplished a major feat in independence while proving this achievement to myself and family.

Perhaps this should be added: Before departing on the trip I had kicked Steve out of instant messenger for angering me over his desire of web cam nudity. Over the years we would kick each other out of instant messenger several times, mostly over the request of nudity but I have been weak and let him back in each time. After the vacation I allowed him back in to say thank you for encouraging the trip. Stupid me, but it's this infatuation of which he is well aware of and uses it to my disadvantage. He plays me terribly and I allow his manipulations. Why Steve though? I know better than to trust men. Perhaps it's the fact that we don't care and play each other to a brutal fault. We are nothing more than nicknames to push around on a flat screen.

The months of May through July found this bored housewife playing on the computer to an extreme now that the rush of traveling was over. With plenty of time on her hands everything else seemed like a restless let down so dull boredom set in with only one outlet—the computer.

Chat rooms were the next best thing to excitement and I could have just as easily been labeled a player back then that played guys. What the heck. The game was played over their weakness from desire of the female sex although it was never sexual release for me like it is for them. From this angle it was more like needing attention or approval that I did not receive at home. Although in my mind the majority of those basic players have nothing over Steve and Brad, a couple of confident well groomed men that lead accomplished lives. If a man has time to waste on the computer during the day then what kind of life does he have? Who the heck am I to talk? *Head hanging in shame* There again this only proves that I have failed, failed to become the total person that I always wished to be.

(Again, contradiction of errors, Steve and Brad chatted during daylight hours too. Well, they are still accomplished in my eyes. They have upwardly steady careers.)

One evening hubby came home from a local bar with something scribbled on a napkin. It was an email address of a computer site for people with web cams. The local female bartender swore that hubby would get an eyeful of t and a. I did have a web cam that was only to be used for sharing with family. Ok fine! Steve and Brad had been flashed and have seen my ample chest. Gee. *Blush*

So what am I struggling to say here? The words struggling to come out are specifically this: I went into that web cam site and received a new education. Its format was nasty and too extreme for my disposition however I chatted with a new person in the room. Ted was divorced with partial custody of one young son, a son I gathered he had little interest in. The man was overweight and not my type in the least but he attached to me quite quickly and I wrongfully allowed him into instant messenger. He professed a strong desire to meet in person. I said no although he steadily persisted day after day. For me it was like 'yeah, yeah, whatever, right'. Why did I continue an acquaintance with someone that I had no interest in? I don't know. It was stupid. Perhaps it was the attention factor again.

Chatting with Ted eventually reached a strange degree. One could readily see that the man had severe underlying issues. Something I wanted nothing to do with. Ted stated that once I came to visit him on the east coast we could go to a certain sex club and he provided an email address to the establishment. I looked it up. Sex club, swinger club, it's all the same. However this particular place looked seedy and dark. Just imagine how many people have had sex in those rooms over the decades. That doesn't seem particularly sensual or romantic but then again it doesn't have to be. In fact it seems mostly dirty and bleak.

There were so called bedrooms with names and themes to sugar coat the attraction. Information was later pointed out by a female swinger that if a sex club has bedrooms with doors it's under an old set of rules and regulations. They do not have to remove the doors and are allowed to continue operating as is. However in the past few years a new law has gone into effect where a sex club may cover the door but not with a solid structure. The implication being that should the law choose to enter the building they need immediate viewing access as to who is in the room. Why would the law wish to enter the club? You decipher that one for yourself . . . criminal intent . . . underage . . . complaint.

During the week I told hubby about Ted and the site. Hey, I teased hubby about having boyfriends. He is well aware that I talk with guys online. Even at a later date I informed my husband that I had flashed Brad while using the web cam and had also asked Brad to join me in the Bahamas. He is even aware of phone sex with Ben and the Christmas necklace of which I paid for. What did hubby do or say about all this revelation? Not much. There was no out and out battle between us finished with an accusing war. It was all calm discussion. He allows me to play since there is little harm in only talking with someone. No bodily contact is made followed by a pleasurable exchange of physical touch. What could he say? He receives attention from petite bubbly strippers every Saturday night to touch and view face to face. Oh, I have got more startling revelations yet to come. Hubby has allowed quite a lot. I believe at this point the question had even been asked whether I could have sex with either Steve or Brad if the opportunity presented itself. He said he couldn't stop me. Women have it easy. They can get sex whenever they want it he says. Men do not have the same luxury. Perhaps true. Quite obviously he thinks about this matter and wishes for the exchange.

After dinner that evening we checked out the sex club's site together. My husband had heard mention of a swingers club near our area. Together we sat at the computer reading about Ted's sex house, the rules, membership and such, and then hubby said search our area for swinger clubs. We searched with little luck. Sure there was one in the state capital but that was too far to drive. End of conversation. This is all I have to say on the swinger club issue for now but my husband's interest was beginning to perk in that direction. He began to inquire from strippers on Saturday night if they knew of any swinger clubs in the local area.

One hot night in July I suffered an unsettling nightmare or possibly dreaded premonition. My mother was also having bad dreams about her eldest daughter at this same time even though she did not have a clue as to our lifestyle. She knew of my interest with Steve and Brad and had even observed Brad's photo but that's all she was aware of, just enough to unsettle her intuitive maternal instincts.

The unnerving dream portrayed a man outside of my bedroom window. I looked out the open window on a dark evening and heard a deep voice reverberate from out of sight, radiating from the ground. Chills ran through my veins as I could not see a face or form. Only the voice resounded with a low, "I'm coming in." Meaning he was going to break into the house with bodily harm being the direct intention.

That was it! I was done with Ted after our two weeks of chatting and avoided him at all costs. I needed to stay off the stupid computer and besides, this story of Algonquian Indians before the Declaration of Independence wasn't going to write itself. The few short months of warm summertime needed to be enjoyed too.

I doubted my sanity now. Playing on the computer was ridiculous, time consuming and depleting my energies for worthwhile projects such as living a meaningful life. My addiction was reaching the level of almost no return as I was losing the ability to truly communicate in the real world. This deep dark hell hole of a life had to change, but how? Remember I said that I hate people. Avoiding people in the real world is easy but getting on with ones life is not so easy. The need to write was there although sadly motivation was evasive. Believe me it's not laziness. Possibly at the time it was only fear of moving forward, uncertain and unable to find meaningful direction.

# CHAPTER 3

Before we proceed to July 24, 2004 there is another instance from last winter that needs to be addressed or seriously brought to light. There was a major occurrence of which I have been holding back from the reader, a slow unfolding incidence that would change our lives down the road, in fact affect many people in many ways throughout the years. This basic conversation took place about the same time that Ben and I were carrying on. It was around that particular Halloween when the stripper nickname came to fruition. The room for those over 40 years of age is where the . . . I was about to say where the bull crap is kept to a minimum although that would be an understatement. It's a site that is a little easier going and laid back with adult humor. I frequented that room quite often back then even though it remains a wee bit too tame for livelier personalities.

This particular meeting took place on a weekend afternoon. Ray said hello to me in the room while suffering through difficulties on his WebTV. He frantically asked for the room operator's assistance in helping to view profiles. The operator quickly replied that he must have a problem with his cookies and to please clean them up and then try viewing profiles. This stranger insisted that I wait while he left to clean up his computer cookies. Upon returning there was still some sort of a problem and he asked for the room operator's help again. I must have waited ten minutes as he struggled with things oblivious to everyone else. Finally he gave up and we began talking in a whisper window.

This unique man began as a complete gentleman, easy to talk with while actually being quite a vivacious conversationalist. Ray has been divorced for many years while his two teenaged daughters lived with their mother at the time. He lives and has grown up in New York State just north of the city in the bustling Hudson Valley area.

Our unfolding conversation flowed with all the new formalities of getting to know someone as I explained my marriage and for how many years and such. We are also about the same age with me being a year and three days older. Two Leos we made loud reference too. Your den or mine!

We added one another to instant messenger over time plus our conversations continued to flow easily. They were never sexual. He stated it was out of respect since the statement was made that I was married. Our talks were just mild adult humor. We discussed our current weather, living, food—he is a good cook too. Although we were born almost 900 miles apart our lives seemed to flow parallel in several instances most likely due to experiences lived through the same generation. It was a breath of fresh air to finally meet someone honest and open on the internet, a true gentleman.

Perhaps at this juncture I should digress again and state that Ben is 13 years younger than me. The generation gap interfered greatly with our personalities and remains the biggest reason we failed to last. Steve, a fiery head strong Aries, is supposedly six to eight years younger. Brad, a steadfast Capricorn with great wit, stated that he is six years younger.

Although Ray and I hit it off well in the beginning something was just missing. It was toward the end of February 2004 when he and I began tapering off. One day while chatting about the difference between chili soup and chili mac we also discussed similar trucks that we used to drive. There was common ground in the mere fact that we enjoyed high energy of four-wheel driving while plowing through deep snow.

Ray was explaining how the truck broke down when suddenly his WebTV froze. The darn interference in instant messenger has been a frustration for a long time. Perhaps one day it will be thankfully replaced with a computer. (It is replaced with a computer now.) Ray abruptly went offline when the signal died.

He and I had hit it off in several ways but something just wasn't hitting the mark. I was at a position where Steve dominated a percentage of my time. The vacation was made and Ray just wasn't a strong point in this gal's playtime so I deleted his name from instant messenger. His nickname continued popping up in chat rooms that spring but I didn't encourage any more contact.

Now let's jump back to the summer of 2004 and late on a Saturday evening in July, 24th to be exact. Of course I was having fun in the popular room and in pops Ray. In time he whispered with a large hello. Loud inquiry needs to be made at this juncture—do all you Nu Yawkers shout?

"Hello!"

"Hi."

"How have you been?"

"Good and you?" I asked.

We chatted that evening for what seems like hours. More photos were eagerly exchanged through the internet. I had never known a bald man with a goatee, the sexy bad boy look. Oh brother, can they look hot in cool dude sunglasses!

And then the discussion suddenly turned to the guys that I had been playing—four boyfriends.

"Can I be your fifth boyfriend? LOL." He brazenly teased.

Ahh gees, just what I needed, another boyfriend. If Ray wished to be another boyfriend then he needed to prove he had what it took so I pushed the envelope. To my startled eyes that were glued to the computer screen Ray quickly accepted the envelope. The man had seemed asexual because he wasn't piggish but boy was I wrong. We flirted heavily that day and spoke on the phone later. Again no phone sex as we were just getting to know one another over again but our emotional and intellectual connection was stronger than before. I had never met anyone like this individual in my entire life. Even though I'm certain he has also never met a stranger in his life this man states that he felt attraction to me from the very first day. I had sent him a respectable photo from our first meeting and he remembers clearly his feelings of magnetism.

His voice quickly grew on me, the tone and the heavy New York accent. He is always upbeat and positive—the eternal Leo optimism propelling forward. All the while Ray teased me about my Midwestern drawl stating that it takes three syllables just to say one word whereas a New Yorker can say the same word with one syllable. He's so interesting to listen to. It's almost as though he is the teacher, the mentor I've been looking for. Ray is knowledgeable about many things including one of my favorite subjects—history. Well certainly. He lives in New England were a great deal of the action took place two and three hundred years ago. His family line is Dutch, Irish, Italian and American Indian.

And Ray also knows women. The guy is surrounded by only sisters and daughters. Perhaps a person might also note this is one large aspect that attracted me to Ray. He knows women. That seems to be a generalized prerequisite of a good man, a family man. If ever someone needed the love and comfort of a good man that would unquestionably go into battle to fight and defend his family and children . . . it was me. I still discuss this issue with my sister over the fact that our father failed us. But Ray is the kind of father that still protects his girls even through the terrible strain of divorce, quite admirable.

Have you ever sat in the distance while watching a small family? We're all well aware of the mother's position nurturing, gathering her group, wiping little faces and hands. But have you ever watched as the patriarch steps forward when the mother can do no more, when her hands are so full that she can no longer be in two places at one time? It is remarkable watching as the father begins to care for, tend to the children with a gentle hand and simply provide assistance to his cherished family. Seeing a man lovingly nurture, support and guide his family is beyond my basic comprehension. Ray was once that man when his family was young.

Two days later we stepped up to another level and had phone sex. Ray stated in reference to the four boyfriends that he knew he was quickly rising up the ladder. It's true as he had blown the competition away, he was perfect. Once Ray entered my life I mostly forgot about the other guys. Well, for awhile. Ray had reached status of number one boyfriend.

We just clicked. We were right where we wanted to be, right where we needed to be. His girlfriend of four years was gone. Well, not totally gone but their relationship was over so he stated. It is true. They were over as their love connection was dwindling to a point of near nothing. She was unable to prove her love which became my benefit as I'm still able to prove love everyday. However they are still friendly to this day and it's completely alright. Lifelong friendships are a good thing to hold onto. I am slowly learning the healthy idea of not burning bridges. Even Ray and his ex-wife remain on a mostly steady keel raising their two precious possessions. We all need people around for support even if it is from old lovers.

You've heard of two peas in a pod? Ray and I are exactly that—two peas in a pod. We finish each others sentences. When one changes the subject the other already knows the bulk of the next topic of where it's going. One day we were discussing apples. I didn't realize that New York is well known for their apple orchards besides Washington State orchards. (Yes, I forgot the story of Johnny Appleseed from grade school.) So we typed words on the screen simultaneously. He typed red delicious while I typed golden delicious. It's a joke that we carry on to this day, but another instance was a little freakier. Mind you Ray and I are almost 900 miles apart and I had never been to New York much less traveled the road he was on. As he drove along we were having a conversation on the cell phone when suddenly he said, "That's a nice house but a little too close to the road."

Stating nonsense I opened my big mouth and asked, "What is it? Blue?"

"Oh my God," was all he said.

"It's blue?"

"Yeah."

What is the percentage of blue houses in this world? My guess is that the percentage is low. Blue?! And why would a person question reference to a color when his statement was about distance?

We laughed on that one. It seems like there are so many other topics that went the same direction of mind boggling coincidence. We can state a line from a song or an old commercial from our generation . . . or scenes taken from an old television show and the other remembers clearly. We remember many creative and colorful things from the 60's and 70's.

Honestly I don't believe in soul mates. That particular phrase seems like a romantic excuse. But kindred spirits possibly do exist. Ray and I definitely have something larger than ourselves to be able to work together so well. Day after day we enjoyed (and still do) this close bond of friendship that is blessed from a higher realm. It has to be blessed from a higher realm because there is no other reasoning.

Perhaps I might be allowed to become silly for a moment (darn, can't blame the Irish ancestors on this one), but there is also an instance where his female neighbor had a dream or flash of a past life. She dreamed that Ray and I were in a horse drawn buggy riding back and forth down the primitive road in front of the their homes. That one still freaks me out. About the same time he had a vivid dream too. Ray was maneuvering a canoe in the freezing cold frantically trying to return to me, only to find that he was suddenly in the middle of a revolutionary type battle. There was also a bear in the dream that kept bothering him. Don't know what the bear meant. Anyway Ray has many colorful and action oriented dreams so who is to know.

The beginning of this fantastic connection with Ray was still a bit of a game for me. The computer was for play and I was married to a grounded personality while stuck in middle of this stagnate little one horse community. Reality was my husband's habitat and responsibilities that were part of our marriage package. We run a tight ship here at home even though I fell into big trouble for not getting chores done and out of the way within a reasonable amount of time. I am a writer was my excuse! I needed to be on the computer to write. This tormented epic adventure of Algonquian Indians before the Declaration of Independence wasn't going to write itself.

"I don't give a crap about your writing," he retorted loudly, "the floors need swept three times a week." And that means moving all the chairs and rugs. "Also, the bathrooms need cleaned once a week." We went round and round about cleaning for months up to a year. I've finally gotten a good routine going now.

In the middle of one heated argument he threatened to throw the computer out the window. My hot Irish temper quickly flared to the surface at that very moment. Dangerously close while face to face the conversation swiftly subsided though. What fool would destroy a thousand dollars over momentary inability to express themselves rationally not to mention my cumulative work of priceless stories. Thankfully the stories are also saved on disk. But that was the second time in our marriage together when I became firm while treading on his solid terra cotta. The first temper flare up had been shown over sweeping the blasted floors back when we newlyweds and this second flare up fell many years into the marriage. He backed off swiftly never to mention throwing the computer out of the window again.

Honestly my husband and I don't fight. We argue though. Sure, who doesn't? He has a loud voice that is difficult to shout over. It's a strong family trait that comes naturally so I bide my time waiting until the volume slowly dies down. Possibly I might say one line in return and then walk away from the heated exchange. His direct to the point common sense over obvious matters rarely misses its mark and is difficult to argue with. I believe both sides should be allowed to hold their ground. There are two sides to every story and each party should be allowed to vocalize their important personal views. Everyone has an opinion and it should be valued whether agreed upon or not. That last line is pure gold. 'Everyone has an opinion that should be valued whether agreed upon or not'. Spread that remark around. The world might benefit from the simple statement.

The second way that we argue is should his ego become bruised he will wander off while moping for awhile, a few hours or up to a day but no longer. A couple of times he has called from work to say 'I don't want to fight anymore'. Sufficient and enough said. We make up. Not passionately. We just make up.

Before moving on to this next juncture in time intricate research needed to be completed first. Some of Ray's old emails were reviewed. Wow, we didn't have a chance but to fall for each other. Our words bounce off one another like diving head first over exhilarating rapids of a water park on a hot summer day. I've come to understand a little about our remarkable connection. Ray doesn't easily fall for my bull shit because he's the only man that can tell me 'no'. Let's rephrase that statement—he's the only man I listen to when told the simple word of 'no'. He sees right through the fruitless excess of excuses and challenges me on each and every level. By now can't the reader see that challenge is a portion of what drives me? Challenge in the real world had frightened the dickens out of me but on the internet I can dish out anything and everything . . . declare something to the world and who is to say whether I am truthful or exaggerating. But Ray sees right through me. He knows me well. (Believe me this story is truthful. It has to be because many will contest this account down to the fine details. It is my therapy, my only chance to see light at the end of the tunnel and move on to the next stage of existence. I am certainly ready.)

Right out of the gate we began this emotional affair quite strongly. Ray called my house as he drove to work in the mornings, every morning, he phoned the house at every break and then we talked again as he drove home from work too. Most every weekday for three or four months there was a creative email awaiting him on his WebTV.

*Hi Baby!!!*
*Welcome home, kick your shoes off, sit back and let me take care of everything.*
*I'll fix dinner, we'll do the dishes together and then rent a movie.*
*After the movie we'll go to bed and make passionate love.*
*Love, Me*

Tell me what struggling divorced man wouldn't adore receiving tender words such as these or imagining his ideal woman? I brought a tear to Ray's eye a few times but not only from elaborate emails. There are other instances too. Ray needed to be loved while I needed a man to appreciate this depth of affection I was capable of offering. This is still difficult to write with so many issues involved that are not completely accessible. Issues like finances and loneliness. More will be revealed carefully as we proceed forward.

Our birthdays are three days apart in the hot month of August. With just a few weeks behind our reconciliation we seriously wondered how to surprise the other with a birthday gift. We asked questions and sizes, quite obvious at this point that someone would receive clothes. However do you know what the funny thing is? While Ray went shopping he called from his cell phone and stated, "You would look good in peachy-pinks." He teased, "Hmm this might look good on you, but no wait I see something else." How many men do you know that go clothes shopping for their girlfriends? Those men are out there. Quite charming I must say.

The day of my birthday I received three knit tops and one pink shirt and two birthday cards. FedEx arrived while we were on the phone and it was such an accelerating rush to tear open the box while talking with him. It was like Christmas morning! I was so excited. Later I went to the computer and used the web cam to take pictures of each shirt with white jeans on. One top was called three-quarter length sleeves, another boob sweater (it was thin and stretchy), a pink short sleeved tee, and a pink blouse. I loved them all. Ray did a great job.

A couple days later his birthday package arrived in New York by express mail. He failed to wait for my company on the phone as he quickly dug into the box, and then called right afterwards stating, "I couldn't wait. Now I know how you felt. And yeah it was just like Christmas!" He loved his two shirts, especially the white v-neck knit tee shirt from JC Penney's. Oh, and the birthday card. Oops, and my white tee shirt that I used to sleep in that was now fragrant with my perfume. It was only after we actually met that

Ray slipped the shirt over one of his bed pillows and slept while hugging it many nights.

Fall came with its usual dimming of daylight hours along with cooler temperatures. It quickly approached just like every progressing year. Time really does seem to move faster and faster. Guess that's what happens when one is having fun and so Ray and I had to meet. I deserved to be with another man while I was still young enough to be vibrant. Sexuality in my house was slipping desperately. My husband did not need Viagra but he needed something besides strippers. Also my resurrecting flirtation with hubby was not working. I needed serious validation that my sexuality did exist and Ray was interested.

A quick note here: Yes I knew the danger of meeting someone from online. I watched the news and heard television reports along with everyone else. There are dangerous men online, killers and rapists, and who's to say that the person someone meets does not have STD's? It's Russian roulette. A little like college perhaps? Or meeting someone from a bar? You discuss these things honestly and openly beforehand. And romanticism of meeting someone new is just that, romanticism—it's not always logical reality or clear thinking. There are a million forms of reality for each and every different person. Be cautious and be careful.

The scheme to meet Ray was highly creative. Coming from me could it be any other way? September the thick plot unfolded as my husband received information that I was going shopping which was the truth of the matter. I did go shopping 50 miles away to the best mall district. Ray talked with me on the cell phone off and on throughout the day as he was aware of the creative story that was transpiring.

It was after dark when I pulled the car into the garage and then went into the house. Hubby had finished dinner by the time as I plopped shopping bags on the dining table and we greeted each other with an upbeat manner.

"I stopped by one of strip clubs this afternoon," I stated.

He was a bit surprised. "You did?"

"Uh huh and I saw Houston again. She sat with me and we talked for a short while." His face carried a curious expression as I explained. "There was also another girl that sat with us the whole time. Her name is Lisa. She's from around there and we just had a couple drinks and talked with the girls."

"She's a stripper too?"

"No, I guess you could say she's a little bi-curious like me."

"Oh."

In hopes that he would buy the story this plot carried onto the next level while feeling out the tempo. "Anyway Lisa and her friends are going up to the state capital and wondered if I would like to go with them. They're going on a three day shopping trip while leaving on a Friday afternoon. Saturday night they'll go bar hopping uptown. A long time ago in college we hit those night spots so I remember the area well."

My husband bought it easily after several more intricate details were revealed and he agreed that I could take this trip with the girls. That night in instant messenger Ray stated 'I guess my name is now Lisa'.

Second weekend in October we were excited beyond belief. Ray called early in the morning from his Dulles Airport layover while I attempted to get the household chores under control. Damn phone stuck to my ear all the time makes working and moving around rather difficult. I can tell him over and over and he still just doesn't understand the aggravation. Sure I enjoy talking with him but there is always a ton of work to do. *Heavy sigh*

I was nervous hoping that every aspect remained covered in this broad and intricate lie. All sticky details seemed to be falling into place. The livestock were fed. The potted plants were watered quickly. Mail was brought in and thrown on the table. My bags were packed and stuffed in the car. This was it. No turning back now. Whew. I began the long two hour drive and hoped my husband didn't come home early to see that I had left by 11:00 am instead of late afternoon as was mentioned before. Oh, and I had prayed that there would be no rain on this day. If it had rained he would not have gone to work and that situation would have only produced another difficulty. A portion of the lie was that the girls were going to drive past our house to pick me up. There is one more elaborate deception yet. I had another lie to cover up as well once my husband arrived home and noticed that the car was missing. Not enough room for five girls and luggage in their small car was the excuse he would receive. Told you I was creative.

The airport was now within sight and the cell phone rang.

"I'm here," Ray says.

"Ok good, I'm on the highway five minutes from the airport. Where are you at?"

"I'm still inside the baggage claim area but meet me outside in the pick-up zone. I'll be on the sidewalk watching for your car."

"Alright I'm not familiar with that area but I'll find it, no problem." A smile was on my face and in my voice. "I can't wait."

"Me too. You're in heavy traffic so I'll let you go. See ya in a few minutes."

The car slowly entered the pick-up area and I eagerly searched the few faces of people . . . and then I saw him. Ray's image was not much different from his pictures. He is not tall like the other men in my life. Walking toward the curb a black satchel strap was draped over his shoulder. He smiled and then approached the car as I slowed to a stop. Parking at the edge of the sidewalk I got out just as Ray came around the back of the vehicle. We were ecstatic and then he placed a big kiss on my lips. Fireworks suddenly went off with a bang and all I could exclaim was 'wow'. He still laughs about that to this day. He also states that he kissed me one more time. My mind must have been clouded at that point.

We got back into the car. Mind you, two people smiling from ear to ear. We just kept glancing to one another while remarking we're really doing this. It was so surreal. I quickly fell into the pool of Ray's big blue eyes. His facial expressions are so animated while his demeanor is upbeat and easy going. I could continue carrying on with adjectives for this awesome man but perhaps I should just stop and carry on to the next scene.

Within 10 minutes from the airport we pulled into the parking lot of the hotel that was reserved for the weekend and we grabbed our bags and went inside. At the front desk I signed for two key cards for room 103 and away we went.

The room was quite adequate for our needs as we dropped the bags at the edge of the room and instantly became embraced in a kiss. A slow and sensual kiss, arms wrapped around one another as we searched for the feel, the energy of the physical person. We already knew each other emotionally and mentally so bodily presence was just a new compounding sensation to pleasure.

As we broke apart Ray asked, "Should I close the curtains?"

Nervousness wasn't a factor although I remained mildly unsure of unfolding circumstances but not about to turn back now, "Sure," I replied. After he closed the curtains we slowly began to undress. My pink shirt came off first. It was one of four that he had purchased for my birthday, and then slowly one bra strap was slid from a shoulder and then the other, teasing him in a slow reveal. 'Mine all mine' he was thinking while relishing in the sight before the white jeans and white thong came off. We made love for the first time and it was awesome, passionate and desiring, hands slowly roaming caressing and exploring. Tempo slowly building to an ardent need and want, demands that needed to be fulfilled, and they were fulfilled beyond measure. With a smile he would remember my words afterward of 'wow, wow, wow'. Laughing to myself while writing, possibly in real life vocalization is not such a strong forte.

Ray stated after our indulgence, "Didn't know what you've been missing did you?"

"Nope, but I knew there had to be more." And validation became complete, I had found it. My sexuality was suddenly off the charts. They say that women in their 40's sometimes find desire as strong as a teenage boy's. If that's the case then I had reached that point. Sexually speaking my 30's had been boring but no longer, the depth, the urgency was astounding and completely fulfilled with this exceptional man.

Ray and I made love twelve times from Friday afternoon to Sunday morning. Yes, actually twelve times. I was just fine but he would recall that he was completely drained. To be totally honest I was not in mood for sex for several days afterward. Sex at home would never compare to the caliber of that weekend either, a feeling that continues lingering to this day.

That weekend was validating in so many ways. I now realize that I am still capable of being the total package of a real woman and learned all this with a special man. We began loving one another with an authentic love that is felt from the heart. I care greatly for Ray, for his health and happiness and for his struggling well being. There are so many days when we wish we could be close to one another for company, for support, just a simple touch or kiss, something that makes us feel whole from deep inside.

That first evening we ordered pizza, breadsticks and chicken wings which were a feast to our ravenous appetite. It was divine and then later while watching a movie we consumed white zinfandel and brownies for dessert. I know that combination sounds quite unappetizing but we were happy together and indulged in the crazy treat.

What was I really feeling at this time? There was a sense of calmness, relaxation and total contentment. It was like nothing that had ever been felt before. Day to day living in the Midwest is so nerve wracking without anyone to calm my vibrant nature, but that weekend Ray and I were one in movement, mentality and contentment. It was similar to being on a vacation but in reality it was a physical affair. We knew this and did not lie to one another.

Saturday noon came around and we finally escaped the room branching out for lunch at a nice food chain. Unexpectedly my cell phone rang while we were in the middle of lunch. It was my husband wishing to talk about things. Ray quietly finished his meal before going outside for a smoke while leaving me time alone with this important phone call.

"I'm alright with the fact you took the car it's no big deal. I just wondered how things are going."

"We're doing fine, just finishing lunch."

"Is Lisa there with you?"

"Yes, but she just went outside for a smoke leaving us alone so we can talk."

"I see."

He spoke quite a bit about his Friday evening at the pub with the guys, and then spoke of plans for Saturday night at strip clubs before inquiring about our intentions.

I continued, "After eating we were going to continue shopping. Then tonight we're taking a taxi downtown to check out the local bars." The reason for the taxi was this: should he ask at a later date how to drive in the center of this city I wouldn't have a clue. It's a complicated city to maneuver through. Also drinking and driving is an issue that obviously everyone should heed.

That afternoon Ray and I continued the outing. We went shopping at a well known department store and then drove to the mall. We walked the mall hand in hand at times and had a total blast. (While re-reading this segment to Ray over the phone he is correcting me. It seems that we did not hold hands as much as I remember. Ray tells me that I have a tendency to take off walking without regard to his presence. He calls this my independent streak because I seem to do everything on my own. It's true. I'm not used to having someone by my side to slow down progress.) But nonetheless Ray and I did enjoy our time at the mall. We also stopped for a Smoothie and a frozen coffee.

But the real kicker of the afternoon was when he suddenly noticed his favorite steak house on the premises. "Oh my God! That's where we're having dinner tonight!" He exclaimed. You know it is true that all Nu Yawkers shout. Just kidding.

We went back to the hotel room, made love again, took a shower together and then got ready to go out on the town for dinner. Back in the car Ray carefully opened his CD case and pulled out Def Leppard's Vault. Behind the steering wheel he put the disk in . . . and then we *rocked*, turned up the volume on the speakers and jammed like crazy. It was such a blast as we knew and sang every song together. Mind you two people in their mid 40's cruising along with young people in their hot little rides, music blaring through the windows while just having a great time. Sigh with a smile on my face. We will never forget that weekend.

Not all details of this sensational weekend need to be revealed and some will just have to rest. Although Ray states this could be a spicy novel in revealing some hot moments. I say no. Shock effect is good in some instances but just not here.

After dropping Ray off at the airport Sunday morning and watching him inch through security I finally left for home. Along the first highway I relished in the memory of our last embrace and kiss. The sensation of his body next to mine remained forever engraved in my psyche. When he settled in at the airport we spoke momentarily on the cell phones with reassurance that each was going to be alright.

"I had a tear in my eye," he said.

"Yeah me too," I replied. We had met. We had taken our relationship to a new level, an intense physical level. It was at this time we actually began falling in love, something that forever changed us.

The long drive home created substantial time to clear the thick fog from my head. This other side of life was completely detached from the reality of day to day living. Emotionally it is easy to come to terms with the fact that I can love two men at once. There remains enough emotional fortitude in my core to propel love into two different directions while not letting either focus overlap. Each man inspires something different, mentally and physically.

The last hour of the drive home slowly found me returning to earth. I was ready to get home and get back to normalcy as well as physical rest. Stepping into the house my husband greeted me with a big smile. He wished to hear all the juicy details of my exciting weekend with the girls. I walked away with some flimsy excuse but he followed.

"Did anything happen between you and Lisa?" He asked with expectations since I had planted juicy bi-curious visions of nude women in his head. I just smiled really big as he stated, "I take it something did happen."

"Oh yeah."

"Did you two make out?"

"Uh huh."

"Once?"

"No, twice and it was awesome."

"So you went down on each other?"

I was not lying, "Uh huh."

"Are you going to give me any details?"

"I'm a little embarrassed about this right now. Could we wait and talk about it later?"

It was later in the day when we discussed the storyline a little more while I created visions of another world. He was extremely interested in the fact that I had been with another woman and now wished to meet her and possibly watch us together one day. In his mind he would observe as she and I aroused each other and he relieved his own needs from the background. Oh brother, I was going to have to let this settle for awhile. In reality shit was about to get really deep. But hey, I'm creative. It's a miracle that this whole mess pulled through with barely a glitch. Or maybe it's the fact that my husband is very naïve.

Of course Ray and I had to meet again. This time I boldly asked my husband if I could journey down south to Lisa's physical home of all places. She supposedly invited me over for a long weekend. My husband got all excited while asking if he could meet us in the city Saturday night, go out to eat or maybe we could join him at the strip clubs. I had some excuse in place. There was a party or something. Hubby was a little disappointed with the fact we would not be able to get together, but oh well.

The next month was November and temperatures were not too cold as of yet. I took a light weight jacket and did just fine. Flying into Stewart airport in Newburgh, New York on a bright and sunny day was simply beautiful. The tall mountain ranges roll along the terrain with many glacier lakes randomly gleaming sunlight back at the plane's window. It was an awesome sight as New York is an absolutely beautiful state. I love New York, but Ray tells me it's what is in New York that I love. Ok fine, you win again sweetheart.

At the terminal in the main hall there was Ray waiting right outside the security doors. Oh, it was wonderful to see him again. We still make reference to my huge smile as I exit those doors every time. It can't be helped. Ray lights up when sees my smile and those smiling Irish eyes. We hugged and embraced in a completely corny and exhibitionist scene while waiting for my luggage and then went for his car.

Ray lives in a very cute cabin-house along a glacier lake in the woods. The area was once even the very hunting grounds of Teddy Roosevelt. The house has three close neighbors as the wooded area is still considered a neighborhood. Their private road is pinned between a large incline of solid rock and woods as well as Walton Lake from the other side. I absolutely love New York and that cute little cabin even though he is about to move closer to work.

First things are always first and yes we made love as soon as we got home. We were in each others arms again, emotions reeling in our togetherness and it felt good. Sex is important and physically needed but would never be as wildly indulgent as four times a day again.

I quickly made myself at home with items strewn about the house but Ray didn't mind. His girlfriend was by his side and that's all that mattered. Then Saturday found us at Wal-Mart shopping for groceries and a much needed electric skillet as the gas stove was not hooked up. We purchased all the items that one would need to fix a pot of hot chili and also pork cutlets that he would roll in Italian breadcrumbs. You know sex is not everything. One enjoys food as well. Or is it that sex makes one hungry? What is it that they say—men enjoy three things: sex, eating and sleeping. In reality Ray and I enjoy cooking too. And talking, talking about anything and everything in this whole wide world.

The chili with cheese on top and crackers to the side was great. We enjoyed dinner at the dining table by the fireplace although there was no fire in the ancient stone structure this particular night. Through the sunroom windows one can watch lights from half mile across the lake sparkle over rippling water. It is just beautiful. Interior lighting was also dimmed that night making it easy to see through the windows. Nothing can compare to that lingering magical evening there with Ray. Well, maybe a different dinner months later when red candles were lit, the fireplace roared and reflections continued flickering from across the lake.

The next day we toured the countryside through New Paltz, the Mohonk area, Stony Hollow and Ashokan Reservoir. We took several photos of the landscape with the camera. In Kingston I met some of his friends and a few family members as well. It was not until late that evening when we arrived home exhausted but still with enough energy to make the Italian breaded pork cutlets.

We crammed so much into that little trip of two and a half days. The phrase 'I love New York' should never be underestimated and now there was a strong hankering for a sweatshirt with that very phrase.

Before leaving that weekend Ray mentioned, "My business Christmas party is the second weekend in December. I wish you could go with me."

"Of course I would absolutely love to come back next month and go to the party with you but that might be pushing things. Last month the October credit card statement contained the motel bill, and now I have to hide this November bill which contains this flight to New York."

It would have been completely suicidal to put another flight on the next credit card bill along with Christmas presents that needed to be purchased for family. But you know me by now—crazy is my middle name.

Of course back home in the boring Midwest hubby asked again about the trip and inquired if Lisa and I had made out as well. Of course we did I assured him completely although he pressured for more information. He wished to meet this woman. Even his friendly strippers remarked that I was being utterly unreasonable with this secrecy of not sharing. They remarked it would only be fair for my husband to watch a sexual performance or possibly join in a threesome. Oh brother! The tangled webs we weave.

Was I totally crazy? Had I lost my mind completely? I had a boyfriend. My husband thought there was another woman in my life. I spoke to each man as though there were nothing wrong with our lives. My head was not spinning out of control. There was no spiraling into a pit of insanity. Ironically there was propulsion forward, ascension boldly crossing all lines of civilized propriety. I was living, living life to the fullest and it felt darn good for a change. One might wonder this question though—what if someone from our hometown found out about our concealed way of living. My husband and I had many secrets to cover from family and friends and no one knew except for Ray while he accepts me for who I am.

# CHAPTER 4

Our lives were changing dramatically due to all the recent tumultuous events. Place the blame on my broad shoulders for living the dishonest lie. I lied to everyone, husband, family and what few friends we remained in contact with. My sister was even made aware of my infidelity from that specific weekend when Ray and I first met. In a daring and audacious move we had called her from the steak house that evening. Of course she was completely shocked along with my godchild that snuck the receiver off another phone to listen in. A year later the kid knows and teases that auntie has a boyfriend. It's not proper for a child to be exposed to such things but this child is an old soul with a strong understanding of this old world that we live in.

Family and friends are understandably able to see that something is not right within this household. Who wouldn't? No one confronted us face to face over any particular issue but it seems that some were talking behind our back. I believe my in-laws can all see something is askew although they say nothing. But isn't it supposed to be communal support when members of a family or members of a church show up at a person's doorstep to check on the health of someone's soul? Thank goodness that hasn't happened though. At that point we might have to check their heart rate after they fall to the ground from over exposure to an explanation of a lifestyle they couldn't handle.

There is a particular instance from one Sunday during lunch at the in-laws when a family member's infidelity suddenly came to light. The wrong doing was physical sex once or twice with a co-worker. We all stood around as one by one each person said, "I forgive you." Over and over each adult spoke the words with little emotion as they reached the end of the line.

A tear or two were shed until the next person piped up, "Well mom, what's for lunch?"

That was all to the remarkable episode. It blows my mind, the simplicity to forgive such an explosive issue. I'm used to gossip continuing for days, months, years and a few persons hold a grudge for an extra year. Just for good measure mind you. (That would be my brother's in-laws.) Guess the gentle people take the easy way out. Not such a bad idea to forgive, forget and get on with matters at hand actually.

But now to get back to the main point here. With all the changes at home sis remarks that I don't call her on the phone anymore just to shoot the bull and she's right. We still enjoy talking on the phone but I am completely preoccupied with my jumbled thoughts. Is this my addiction? Men being the addiction? Sure. So what happens when both a husband and a wife no longer care for their marriage vows due to their addictions? The obvious downward slide stands firmly in place.

Do you remember that time when I had hit the kitchen cabinet door and saw stars? I had also told my sister that I was finished with this area. I was finished with this community, finished with this county that we live in and also surrounding counties. I was finished with this state of the union located in the boring Midwest. If a nice gentleman from the east coast might come along with children or grandchildren I would not think twice about moving on with my life. I only wanted to live happily ever after in the long run. Together we could watch the children grow up. We would cheer for their teams that they cheered for, attend the plays that they performed in, go to their ballgames, and simply support them as they matured. Of course this community in the Midwest has the same existing attributes but these kids don't need me. They barely notice my existence much less their parents barely acknowledge my interests. These overly gentle natured people could not care less in placing concern upon my curiosity of land, country and national interests. I have tried. The time for trying is now finished. I can no longer go on this way.

The ironic thing is that Ray lives on the east coast and has children that seem interesting. He has a very bright older daughter and the younger child is the same age as my godchild. These girls say hello while using my name! These girls smile unlike my in-laws that when one enters the room they smirk pretense of a grin as if they have been plowing in the field all day.

It sounds as though I am ready for divorce but strikingly in contrast I am not. Security is a very strong factor in a person's existence especially in the form of adequate health insurance and paid off loans, etc. We all need that secure nest egg for retirement as medical costs seem to only rise as we grow older. I have that security with my husband. Ray can not provide this type of protection for me at this time much less for him self and I worry about the quality of his life as we advance toward the future. His girls will struggle to make their way. The oldest knows this and is working very hard to earn a living. She most certainly is going to make it. She's living a good life with her supportive boyfriend by her side. Just keep plugging away. This is what life is all about.

So far this account has been way too easy, so let's make things a little more complicated by returning to the lying exploits of a woman's addiction to men. Throwing toxic ingredients into the cauldron bubbling over with green mirth let's call this complication Steve.

Chatting this fall was still enjoyable especially when Ray joined me. His humorous personality is quite entertaining to most everyone, a gallant persona as a ladies man doesn't go unnoticed and I happily share his bold nature with other women. No problem as Ray assures that he is faithful to only me. Gratefully he is faithful although I cannot say the same for myself. Does the saying 'once a cheater always as cheater' have to be true? I certainly hope not but shiver at the overwhelming implication.

In this timeline of November and December 2004, most mornings Steve would show up by 10:00 am or a little later. The man was so predictable along with his strong personality that could be seen coming a mile away. There are instances of his nasty demeanor as he attempted to jab a wedge between Ray and I while seeing how far he could push us. In the chat room Ray would become exceedingly angry while cutting the lawyer down with harsh comments that created ridiculous drama. Remember I was completely infatuated with the lawyer seeing that he could do no wrong. Even when he told the room that I was cheating on my husband. What a little fool I am.

Behind all this ridiculous drama blowing up on the exposed public podium Steve and I remained very calm while whispering in the background. In one instance Ray was in a complete and massive upheaval while Steve whispered to me, "Go give him some lovin' and calm him down." Quite an honorable and logical thing to say.

Another example is when I told Steve in whisper, "Ray is getting a headache from arguing with you."

The words were typed on the screen quite quickly, "Give him a blow job and he'll be fine."

I was shocked, "Well gee," I stated before rapidly turning the computer off.

Ray was well aware that Steve and I were talking in whisper. We call it my attraction to challenge and most times I *will not* back down from verbal force. The only time I back down is if there are chores to do or someone's livelihood is on the line. Ray loves me for who I am along with my head strong ways. He puts up with all the stupid drama. He also enjoys the theatrics quite a bit too, must be our leonine showmanship thing.

I have to make one more remark for what it's worth. Young English blokes can be very nasty while bashing gays and someone's mama. I have shocked and shut down these young mouths too. Guess that totes the phrase 'one can make a sailor blush'. Fun is fun and so is bold and daring. Am I a bully? Probably so.

One morning a new nickname showed up. This person typed greetings to the room before whispering me. That was the first clue as to the intriguing man behind the dark mask. This nickname was new to the site that particular day which is the second clue. Steve's method of operation was the same and I knew instantly.

"Hi."

"Hello."

"Perhaps the lady would like to chat?" Another clue revealing Steve's personality remains with the fact that he uses the word 'perhaps' while asking a question.

"Sure, what do you look like?"

"5'9" Dark hair, brown eyes," he stated quickly and then failed to ask for my image. A chatting guy never fails to ask for a woman's statistics. That's a biggie, a major starting point in a male's seduction, and if it's not the seduction package they are looking for then it is at least curiosity.

I inquired, "May I ask what you do?"

"Construction, Miami, Florida."

"Homes, bridges, high rises?"

"Sure," he replied after a long pause.

What a deficient story teller! He was not into construction. It's a known fact that guys in a particular career never fail to narrow the field if not brag about their prowess. Bragging not being a bad thing as it is confidence and a confident man is desirable.

I asked, "Are you sure you're in construction? There are no high rises in Florida."

"Sure there are."

"Yeah right." I know that my swift judgment was wrong but due to hurricanes one would think of coastal weather factors.

Steve and I spoke for a couple of hours that morning while he continued working. We were spending long hours chatting on the computer day after day (not always with each other of course) and I stated out of concern 'please don't let chatting interfere with your career'. He assured in typical one liner dialog that chat was not interfering. One can only wonder about the harm of constant distractions. I fully understand the frustrating implication.

"Would you like to meet me?" Steve suddenly asked under the cover of this new nickname.

I was floored! Steve actually asked me to meet him. I re-read the screen over and over. Didn't he realize that I was practically his stalker? Do you know how many attorneys reside in New York City under the same first name while born under the same month and year as this enigma of a figure? Several. The first one that I found even had been a professor of creative writing. Steve said he enjoys my creativity. Could this man with the Irish sir name be Steve? That handsome man even had the same dark Irish look of my great uncles. Oh well, I'm such a ridiculous dreamer.

I needed to give an answer to the previous question. "What do you drive?" I asked instead.

"Land Rover."

"What color?"

"Blue."

"If you wish to meet me then make it Friday afternoon at the grocery store in my hometown."

He paused. "You prefer meeting in public?"

"Sure."

"In the vegetable section?"

"Sure."

A large amount of time passed as he worked or answered the phone before posing the next question, "What would you do if a man pressed against you from behind?"

I smiled while imagining Steve's flirtation. "I would squirm my backside against him."

"What if you felt a banana between your legs?"

Sigh. He was playing hard ball again, pardon the pun. He knew (knows) how to get to me. I fail to see the set up and then suddenly *bam* the punch line hits me upside the head. But that's what I like about Steve and why he must be a very good attorney. He knows how to set someone up for the fall. With a criminal mind I find that manipulation totally fascinating and just can't get enough of it.

At the end of this conversation and before parting I suddenly stated using his real name, "Take care Peter." (Peter is not his real name of course.)

"Who's Peter?"

"You."

"You must have someone else in mind."

";)" I gave him a wink and then left.

Steve and I chatted hard and heavy during that November and December. I hate to reveal this but must reveal everything to be forgiven for my sins. He asked for pictures as usual and I finally gave in. They were sexy but tasteful photos—nude, taken by the web camera. Ray did not have a clue about this for the longest time until I told him. Of course he was hurt and could not believe that I had behaved so foolishly, but he forgave me quickly. Ray also made me promise to never do it again. I failed to be faithful to my boyfriend and yes Steve received more at a later date. (Thoughts of blackmail Steve? I think not as I've revealed all now. Hubby has been made aware of this matter too.)

Slowly from out of the woodwork other girls are coming forward stating that they think Steve is an intriguing man but I am happy to find out he continually asks them for photos too. As if this could provide any comfort. His colors are showing big time now. Steve is a player that plays women for favor of sexy photos. That's not very nice mister. Did you know this trait easily labels a man as a 'player' and a 'pig'?

In messenger Steve's method of playing hardball was finally wearing thin so I tried avoiding messenger and spent most of the time conversing in the chat room. One afternoon another new nickname came onto the screen. This male had the same method of operation and I saw my vehement friend written all over again but was still not quite sure.

"Hi, care to chat?"

"Sure," I replied.

"Asl?" he asked meaning age, sex, location.

"42, female . . . and u?"

"27, male, FL."

"Oh sorry, you are too young for me."

"Do you not like younger guys?"

"I don't chat with them, too much generation gap."

"But I like older women."

"Ok I'll chat with you for a bit." But only because I was searching for clues denoting that this was the lawyer. His method of operation was severely different but there was something about this guy. I couldn't put a finger on it. Maybe it was the choice of words and how he formed them.

We communicated for a short time as I explained my boyfriend and a little about my life but suddenly this person turned on me. For Steve to transform his character to such a sharp degree, well, this could not be. The previous personality of the lawyer was too basic, too carnal, but he was pulling this charade off pretty good as I began to doubt my instincts. Oh, it was Steve alright as I found out at a later date. Pondering the situation—possibly he had someone with him in the room, a friend or someone to put a verbal slant on the game.

Our conversation was rapidly dying in this rudimentary game of ugly seduction. I swiftly refused to find common ground to continue with this stupidity. Steve failed to portray a young man with any believability. He was not bubbly enough or arrogant enough in portrayal of a younger person. Young guys are very talkative while wishing to discuss cars, music or their prowess with women.

And then suddenly this person rudely stated, "Well just go fuck your guys!"

How startling! He had never been this rude before so my response was quickly typed, "Go fuck yourself you do it well!"

That was it. Engulfed in anger I hated Steve's guts. He was such a creep! I hated him for leading me on. I hated myself for allowing him to treat me this way! If ever there were a way to effectively get even I certainly would.

The next day I unblocked Steve from messenger. We were going to have it out once and for all and for the first time in ages he came online. Shockingly he was in his office.

"☺" I put up a smiley face.

"Hello." Steve never used the word hello and then the words came onto the screen, "Who is this?"

"Steve?" I typed the inquiry.

"No this is his assistant."

One day the lawyer was off in a meeting and I actually did communicate with his assistant. "I believe we chatted once before."

"No, I don't think so. I'm new here."

"Oh."

"Who are you," she asked.

I still wasn't convinced that this was not Steve. He had proven capability of being very sly. We had just exchanged harsh words yesterday and I would not put it past the man to implement a new game. Possibly it was wrong of me to assume anything at all and instead gave this poor lady a terrible shock. Whatever, it was fun.

To answer her question I replied, "A friend."

"Like a pen pal or something?"

"Yes." *Rolling my eyes with sarcasm*

Several seconds and minutes past at times during the conversation, the assistant stated that she was updating his schedule in the computer and then the woman suddenly asked, "How well do you know him?"

"We know each other pretty well."

"Intimately?"

Hmm, well possibly the answer could be yes in a way. He had shared knowledge of his desires and prowess with women. I began playing hardball just the way Steve liked it—completely socially unacceptable. "What does your heart tell you?"

The other end paused before typing, "My heart tells me to stay very far away."

I had to laugh, "LOL"

Somewhere along the line this conversation changed and I asked, "What does he look like?"

"Oh you two have never met?"

"No."

She responded, "I can't say. That would be breach of employer confidence."

Crap, I failed to get any information out of the assistant with that inquiry so I directed the conversation again, "What's it like to live in the city?"

"In high rises we have to watch out for peeping toms."

Stupid me. I failed to get the joke at first and responded, "Well around here we don't think much about that although I do leave the dining room curtains open at all times."

"LOL" She laughed.

"Do you know when he will be back in the office?"

"Hang on, be right back, telephone."

I waited and wondered. This person probably was the new assistant. Method of operation or method of chat was definitely different. She was wordy and nice. That's not to say Steve was not slick enough to execute a new personality but I just couldn't believe he was capable of being this different. No matter, one way or the other I needed to get even with this man for yesterday.

"Sorry about that," the assistant stated, "Can I help you with anything else?"

Could she help me? Hmm, this was way too easy. How we slid onto the conversation of men I don't recall however she went along with lightly bashing men on a delicate scale. I told her of a certain one yesterday that had been insulting and rude.

"Don't you just hate that," she remarked.

"Yes, but I told him off. I told him to 'go fuck himself because he does it well' LOL."

"Oh," she replied startled.

"Yes." I waited for Steve to intervene if it was actually him but the deed failed to happen. I had startled the gentle lady and she tapered off quite quickly. At least maybe, just maybe she would tell her boss about the strange woman in the computer. Ha! I hope she did! Although she probably felt too guilty about talking with her boss' lady friend to mention any word of the encounter. C'est le vivre.

This up and coming festive Christmas season was an unwanted chore just like the year before. Oh how I hate the holidays and family get togethers. This same saying is repeated every year as fewer decorations are pulled from the attic or displayed on the walls. Last holiday season my boyfriend Ben had given such a rush of new feelings that I barely got the Christmas tree up much less decorations around the house. The radio failed to even utter a tune of the season. This year there were so many things franticly cluttering my mind along with another trip planned to New York, although this one would be short from Friday night to Sunday morning. Ray was now working second shift in his department and would be able to pick me up at 10:30 that evening from the airport.

Three days before the flight to New York I was communicating with Steve on the computer when he asked out of the blue, "When where?"

"What!" I exclaimed.

"Care to act out some of your fantasies?"

"Are you saying what I think you're saying?" My heart was beating very fast now.

"Would you like for a man to approach from behind?"

"And whisper in my ear?"

"When where?"

I could see the wide grin on his face as he played me. Oh, the little devil must have been having a field day now. Steve was out of town and in Chicago, smack dab in the middle of the Midwest and a five hour drive away from me.

I relayed to him the name of my nearest city with a major airport, the same city that I would be driving to in three days to fly to New York. Oh, how I hated that drive back then. But to meet Steve I would drop anything and everything, even life itself to drive that unpleasant drive in an instant.

"Hotel?"

Oh my gosh! How far was he going to take this? Could he be completely serious now as I quickly grabbed a brochure of the city? Checking hotel listings I typed, "Holiday Inn, Adams Mark, Drury Inn, Hyatt . . ."

"Hyatt. Phone number?" He received the 800 number and then asked while dialing the number, "Jacuzzi?" We had shared a sexy scenario of a man and woman once before nude while in a Jacuzzi.

"Sure if one is available."

"One bed or two?"

Honestly I do not remember my reply but perhaps Steve would remember. This idea of meeting him was scary enough as I was uncertain but invigorated at the same time. He was a strange man with a strong personality, totally superior to mine. A few moments past in the exchange before he stated, "No Jacuzzi."

"That's ok."

"What will you wear?"

The conversation slowly fades from here. I gave him my cell phone number and we agreed to meet online again in the morning before venturing any farther. There was a slight chance that this might fall through due to the case he was working on.

That night I created another deception for my husband. It was a rough deception that I would not have complete control over. The fictional occasion was to spend the night at my sister's house, besides it was Christmas and we needed to spend some time together. He didn't put up much resistance even with the fact that I was going to be gone in three days over the weekend as well. I quickly packed a carry on that evening and hid the bag. I hid the bag because you know the phrase 'out of sight out of mind' has real meaning. The less my husband thought about this added trip the better. I was riding precariously high on a tall limb now while spinning out of control. If I fell I didn't care. If anyone found out . . . I could not have cared any less. At least Steve's identity would finally be known. I would see him and hear the sound of his voice. It's the only thing that mattered.

What were my thoughts during all this activity? Honestly now, I don't believe that I was thinking much at all. Every move and every action that was performed needed to be in tuned with my husband's thoughts, or with maintaining the close knit relationship with Ray, or in considering Steve's response to created situations. I was living three different storylines all at once. I could do it. I was an actress portraying a wife, a girlfriend or a love starved woman. There was held a bit of pride while knowing not just anyone could pull this off, could deflect the truth so convincingly. I failed to see the process as lying but just manipulating situations to coincide with my wishes to get what I wanted. I felt spoiled and blessed at the same moment. You ask self centered? Yes, big time! A criminal mind? Possibly. Am I dangerous? I don't know, perhaps only to this physical person that resides within this physical core.

The fateful day arrived. So what was the esoteric feeling at this time? Was the sensation excitement, challenge of the dare, possibly feeling evincible to all aspects of the world? Evincible to what I must ask now. Steve had shown tendencies of abusiveness, disrespect and rudeness to women in general, but while riding high on this feeling of invincibility there was a sense of dangerous abandon. I could deal with any man that I came face to face with and it would be on my very own controlled terms as well.

The lobby was grandiose with lofty ceilings. Checkout loomed to the right as I entered the building. A long registration desk glistened shiny mahogany while trimmed with rare ebony. Wearing tight white jeans with a thong underneath while donning a flattering cashmere sweater I strolled up to the counter. Gently leaning onto the wooden ledge I quietly asked a question to the person on duty, "Any messages for Lisa Travis?" The strap of my compact purse abruptly slipped from a shoulder as I shifted upon three inch stilettos and I hoped he was watching.

A large sitting area opened at the edge of a rattan partitioned wall complete with palm trees not native to the area. Designer carpet rounded the large expanse with seating areas grouped across the dark red floor covering. I searched a few faces not knowing what he looked like although certain we would have no difficulty finding each other. One man was shielded from behind a newspaper. I studied the fine textured clothing and the height of the man. It was him. I knew it was him. Tall with sandy colored hair and hazel eyes he had initially told me although I could not as of yet see his eyes.

Steve had wanted to surprise me. He had wanted to find me alone and approach from behind and then whisper something sexy in my ear. Slowly our fantasy world would unfold. It would unfold as I was physically backed against the elevator wall, and then in the privacy of our room. What would I do if a man pressed me against the wall? Two answers—either the man is willing or he plays hard to get. A strong woman always gets what she wants when reaching for it. And he asks what does a strong woman want? She wants a mentally strong man equal in sensuality. The deep voice then resounds while asking does the woman know how to please a man? Yes, there is nothing sexier than the powerful sound that a man makes when he cums. He rapidly fills her with his power and energy as they are merged together as one.

I approached the man shielded from behind the newspaper. "Hi my name is Lisa Travis."

He glanced up nonchalant, "Excuse me?"

We spoke nothing for a moment as I studied sparkling hazel eyes as he fought back a grin. Oh the tall gentleman was poised and polished. The man reeked of confidence, fortitude and self assurance. There resided inner power in his physical being, strict control of emotion and authority in his ability to move mountains if so inclined. As much as I desired interview with a man surrounded by these qualities I had no right to be here. We had nothing in common.

"Sit," he spoke callously without pretense. After taking a seat he asked, "So where do you want to take this?"

"I only wanted to meet you, to see what you look like, to hear the sound of your voice."

"You like?"

I smiled but looked away from mere modesty. "Yes, but we have nothing in common."

"We don't?"

"No."

"You're having second thoughts now? Afraid?"

I was afraid of rejection. Was I actually afraid of his power? Perhaps so. I admire his ability as it is something I have very little of and desire the extraordinary trait of influence and command. Yet we failed to have anything in common. I was just a Midwestern girl . . . common, ordinary, plain . . . and then it all fell apart, this dream that I had the morning before Steve and I were to meet.

But the dream was quickly dashed aside as the bright sun rose in the east. The dawn arrived with a strong sense of excitement with a gentle nudge to get things moving. I couldn't wait for my husband to get out of the house so that the ball could get rolling. With bags packed I went online. That morning I stepped into the chat site hoping that Steve would be on time. I waited and waited but he didn't show.

At the time when Steve had portrayed a Florida building contractor he had given me an email address. Of course he wanted photos at the time of which I supplied two old ones that he had already seen but this is neither here nor there. All this time I had kept that email address. It was a live address and a valid way to contact Steve since he blocks emails in instant messenger. I quickly sent a note hoping that Steve would reply before noon. Within a few short minutes of receiving the letter he came online.

"Hi." I quickly typed.

"Yes?"

"Are we still on?"

"I'm in a meeting."

"Oh." I waited for a bit letting him take control of the next line, especially if he was busy in a meeting.

"What are you wearing?" He asked.

"I'm getting ready to jump in the shower."

"Nude?" Steve playfully inquired.

"No."

"Would it not be more comfortable?"

"Well, yeah, in the shower."

"Not what I meant."

"Oh, I know what you meant."

There was a long pause before he abruptly typed, "I've got to go."

"What! Are we still on?"

"I've got to go."

"But my bags are packed. Does this mean you can't make it?"

Another long pause before he typed "Can't make it."

I sighed completely dejected before quickly typing, "Well I guess I'll just go unpack my bags. Bye." His name disappeared from the screen. That was it, that was all to our amazing chance of meeting.

Abruptly jumping ahead to February 22, 2006 how completely and utterly amazing is this ironic sequence of events. This very same week while typing the story I was subsequently played by Steve again in a similar manner. It's incredible that if Steve only knew how his judgment coincides with my thoughts at times. This is not the first instance. Fate? With Steve I doubt that foolish fate has anything to do with it.

I am home alone this week in February and Steve set me up for a meeting in the same city but nearer to the airport this time. This little fool's heart raced frantically in anticipation as we quickly typed words across the screen. Alas only to end with a certain request of a nude photo.

"No." I said.

"Bye bye then," he replied.

Those three simple words had hurt my feelings so bad. "Wait," I pleaded, "were you serious or not?" He failed to answer. Must I have everything spelled out? Am I this stupid? I guess it's true. Rejection remains supreme. Deep down inside I realize he is only playing me but I actually wanted that meeting.

Early this morning I deleted Steve's primary nickname from my instant messenger. My phone number is now posted so that it can be read from his backup nickname which he rarely uses. He will not call.

6:15 pm. Steve closes down shop after 6 but is still in his office several evenings except Friday. This evening has now ended on a completely stupid note. Late in the afternoon I changed the posted telephone number to instead read 'Steve is a sadistic pig'. He has since employed a woman most likely his assistant to place a crank call of which I quickly hung up on. (Perhaps the reader is rolling their eyes now or possibly laughing their ass off. I don't blame you.) Oh, how I hate Steve the sadistic pig.

This is so cold and callus. How dare he reduce me to reckless abandon from all logic and make me wonton of something I cannot have! Why would a man spend so much time trying to hurt and demean another? On several occasions I stated that I enjoyed chatting with him for his mind, wishing to learn from this vast knowledge that he so proficiently bragged about. Although he repeatedly states 'yeah right' it remains true. I would definitely enjoy having a mentor, I've dreamed of having a mentor. And it is certain that he carries knowledge from career and from traveling that someone could learn from. Imagine the things he could teach me about New York City, Times Square, unique restaurants and fine cuisine, brilliant lights on display during nights on Broadway, holidays in the city, decorated department store windows at Christmastime and the famous Macy's parade. My time was spent wishing to get to know a brilliant personality, one that turned on me. Enough said. Alas, I *am* this stupid. This compulsion for the non-brilliant one has got to stop! And I do believe that my compulsion truly is slowing down at this point. There is nothing left for us to say, remark or discuss with one another. I am nothing more than a tramp in his eyes, one that cheats on her husband so he says. Walk a mile in my shoes buddy! You are far from perfect either.

As calm rational logic returns to reason Steve thoroughly understood what I wanted. Why couldn't he calmly tell me no? At any point in time he could have set things straight by simply stating it wouldn't be a wise choice, its best that we never meet. Brad had firmly set conditions down early on and we knew where we stood. My common sense obviously lacks in many aspects because there are so many things to hide, but Steve does not handle the art of communication on the computer very well either since he hides behind a thick veil. That veil makes it difficult to have a conversation to share thoughts or hints of day to day living. A simplistic answer or comment could do wonders for a complicated series of ridiculous events. Why couldn't he simply state 'Lisa, no! Now get over yourself and realize that when I say no I mean no.'? I would've listened, I would have completely understood, smiled and then asked for the 'next topic please'.

# CHAPTER 5

Reality is Ray's physical presence. Second week of December 2004 Ray and I had been together (dating) for over four months now. We had physically been together two separate weekends and this upcoming weekend was to be our third meeting. A rush of excitement built in our veins as usual. Preparations and plans fell into place easily as I was becoming an old pro at planning and executing what needed to be accomplished for fantastic secret getaways.

Late in the afternoon the garage door went down as the car pulled onto the street right before hubby got home from work. That winding drive to the airport was now becoming easier by familiarity and I parked the car in the same airport parking lot. Sitting comfortably in the airport terminal waiting for the plane none of the passengers had a clue. We didn't know what was transpiring, but then we waited and waited. It was late! My first road block! I had the cell phone and called Ray.

"The plane is late!" I cried.

"How late are you going to be?"

"I don't know. The plane isn't here yet. They say Philadelphia has fog that's setting all flights back a couple hours." It was getting very late in the evening and my second flight was to be the last one out of Philadelphia going to New York in a noisy turbo prop.

"Hmm," Ray was right there with me. "Maybe another airline has a flight going out."

"Ok, let me check and I'll call you back."

I foolishly left this wing of the terminal and walked all the way to the other end of the large building. My suitcase was already checked in as I lugged my heavy carry-on through the halls. But it was all to no avail. There were no more flights going out this evening from any other airlines and I returned to my waiting area to call Ray again.

"I'm stuck here. I guess they will put me on the first flight out in the morning if nothing else happens."

"Oh brother." This was creating a difficult situation all around. Home was 20 miles away for Ray. His car needed to go into the shop for repairs and we were going to rent transportation once I arrived. This meant was that Ray didn't have a way to get home that night and he asked, "Can you call the car rental center and see if they will release the car to me?"

"What's their number?"

Things only got more complicated. I struggled with calling the car rental company. I didn't have a reservation at the time. They were capable of taking my credit card number over the phone for the reservation but Ray would still not be able to take possession of the car. They needed to physically see the credit card. Exasperated, Ray worked the situation from his angle trying to get someone from work to supply their credit card so that he could acquire the rental car. Nope, no one would bite on that. He was stuck at work. I was stuck at the airport.

Finally our stalemate broke a little as my flight came in and I made it to Philly. It was very late in the evening, midnight or something and I called Ray again.

"I've made it."

"Yeah, I watched your flight come in on flightview.com but honey you just missed your flight into New York. You could've made it."

"What?!" I was very tired and very pissed now.

"Didn't the stewardess inform you of connecting flights?"

"No they didn't say a thing this time! Dammit!" And I failed to ask the attendant. That's a big lesson that I've learned since this mishap. Always ask questions beforehand if you do not know connecting flights or what gate number you're going to leave from. I understood the processes but at this late hour it was getting difficult to think clearly now.

That restless night was spent in the front lobby of the Philadelphia airport along with a few other stranded passengers. We suffered in silent misery while curled up in uncomfortable seats. Every ten minutes a pre-recorded announcement went off to 'please protect your valuables and bags by keeping them with you at all times'. Those messages still irritate to no end. That was one long night. Curled up in the chair that was connected to a series of seats I relaxed the best way possible until the kid on the other end moved and jiggled the whole contraption. At one point I took off my shoes and moved to the floor with the carryon tucked under my head. So did the kid. I lost track of an hour and a half, guess I fell asleep then. Five o'clock in the morning I found a restroom and brushed my teeth, freshened up as well as reapplied makeup and felt a little better for the worse. Undeniable fact smoldered under the surface I was very excited about seeing my boyfriend again, adrenalin was riding high.

That morning Ray was able to freshen up and take a shower. Lucky him. He went to a local hotel and spent the night although I felt bad about that too. Ray did not have the funding to spare on hotels and taxis and such. However we both survived.

Saturday morning he met me at the airport. Smiling as always when I come through those doors, a reflection of my own beaming smile. Don't move I tell him, wait right there. He's always waiting right there and then we hug and kiss and make a wonderful sappy scene. We signed for the rental car and drove home to the little cabin in the woods where we fell into bed together.

This particular weekend turned out to be one crazy whirlwind of a ride. After making love we took a much needed nap and then got up and showered together. That afternoon we went shopping for Ray's new black dress slacks and crisp shirt that he would wear to the party that evening. Everything that man and I do together is enjoyable. Ray purchased two different ties, a beautiful black and grey tie with a hint of red in it and also a Christmas tie with a music box inside. Yes, he wore the musical Christmas tie that evening. Oh gee, my party animal.

The dressy function was at a private estate in the mountains, near West Point. It's quite a charming old house that was built around 1900. The simple farm estate is equipped with banquet facilities for large parties and a wet bar near a cozy fireplace in what was once a drawing parlor.

Upon arriving we walked around the lawn to the sidewalk and onto a curved front porch. On the smoke break front porch I began to be introduced to Ray's co-workers. (My wedding ring was not on.) Everyone seemed so congenial, smiled and asked where I was from, said 'nice to meet you' and congratulated Ray on his fine quality of one woman. My boyfriend beamed with pride and I beamed from his leonine pride as well.

Inside the old farmhouse I was introduced to more of his friends, bosses, co-workers and their wives and felt genuinely welcome. Although nervous I smiled and seemed to be well accepted by this new group of diversified people under the title of Ray's girlfriend. Ray was (and still is) well liked and admired by this group. He is a people person, very intelligent, bold and a leader in his own right. This shy little Midwestern girl felt such a rush of freedom. This was so validating while proving that I *can* exist outside in this huge vast world but what helped the most was Ray's personality since he can loosen up my shy nature. When I'm in his presence humanity is not such a fearful thing, he holds my hand, encourages and paves the way for me to step forward with confidence.

I need to ask something quite seriously at this point in the tumultuous learning process. What is so wrong with me that I cannot be validated in my own community? I want to scream at these people 'Why can't you people accept me for who I am, for what I am, and for this head that sits squarely upon these two freakin' shoulders?! Am I such a freak that no one can understand?

Or is it that they are narrow-minded and unable to understand and accept one woman who knows her own mind. Perhaps I am to strong willed for the community. Who knows?! I ask while blindly lashing out at four walls.

Believe me I understand irrational temperament is due to my shortcomings as well as circumstances in life. And one should not bellow and blame the way that we do. There is psychological explanation even for capricious emotions. Ray just states that my bold personality does not coincide with my community. It must be partially true. Possibly my husband is unable to hold his wife's hand, encourage and pave the way due to his backward upbringing. To simply state he is unable to encourage me out of my shell due to his shy shell of an existence.

The party progressed favorably that evening. While maneuvering through hors'duevres in addition to the bar I met office personnel and technical mechanics to small aviation jets. This diversified group hailed from many areas of the country, not just New York but from all over the United States. One couple had also lived in my area for a short time. Remarkably they had only good things to say about the area as they enjoyed their short existence there. Well, they lived in Indianapolis. I would feel more at ease living near a city as well.

For dinner that evening we enjoyed a delicious buffet of lasagna and prime rib, and for dessert we would recall my brownie with ice cream along with Ray's cherry cheese cake which he and some close fellow workers made loud reference to. I still think Nu Yawkers can be quite noisy and I like it. We enjoyed one another's company from the congenial and entertaining table that we sat at. One wife was a nurse. From college days I remember nurses aren't shy when it comes to discussing practically anything. This one proved no exception to the rule while sitting next to the confident receptionist. Not all women were dressed to the hilt in glittery black dresses with strappy heels, some were dressed up and some were casual. I felt very comfortable in black dress slacks with dressy heels and a sexy sweater trimmed in faux mink.

The evening finale capped itself off with music provided by a disc jockey. My first dance with Ray was a slow one and it was great even though I must say with a giggle he requested 'please let me lead'. But hey! I'm not the first girl he has asked to give way. Ray needs to take quicker control so that the girl doesn't have the chance to begin leading. I am just teasing him now. Ray is all man. But that slow dance was nice, holding one another close, feeling his warmth and energy along with those kisses.

By eleven o'clock the party began to quickly fade. We left as well since early morning would come way too soon. We were running on dying fumes by now from little sleep the night before and adrenalin from the rush of being together. Back in the small cabin at the lake we were romantically in each other's arms again. It was sensual and slow with our warm skin pressed together, caresses were just right. This time I told him I was riding the edge, I was about to orgasm. My body froze for a moment and then I exploded so incredibly hard, euphorbia spiraled through my veins. Ray and I were both amazed while this only increased the intensity of his pleasure. He came within seconds and then we snuggled into our warm nest for a few hours sleep.

The alarm was a harsh irritation at five o'clock in the morning. I jumped in the shower quickly and Ray slowly joined me right before I got out. He was exhausted and the pressure shown as stress on his face. This weekend was way too much of a whirlwind for Ray to take. I managed alright with little sleep. Guess I was totally pumped up for this trip and the party as well knowing the validation that would transpire. I was not disappointed in the least even with the rotten start from being stranded at the Philly airport on Friday night.

Ray, still exhausted and struggling, drove me to the airport that morning before returning home for his long nap in the afternoon. It would be five months before we would see each other again. We knew the harsh cold winter would be a long one. But we have a connection, a love that is very strong and grew only stronger from this trip.

Being home alone during cold months is dangerous for some people. Or for lively women should I say? The winter is for boredom. The winter is for playing. The winter is for jacking around with a jerk named Steve. Secretly we sit in our chairs or at our desks and think of how to arouse the others dander. The wintertime is for creativity and for playing hardball and seeing how well one can knock the other from the comfort of their leather chair. And by the way Steve, get your feet off the desk. You're scuffing the polish. Just kidding, it's understandable that runners need to prop up their feet every chance they get.

"Hi," Steve asked of this new lady in chat one day.

She was a beautiful woman. Connie was a tall leggy blonde with long flowing tresses and from her photo she was of model proportions. Oh, the girl was also single with a sharp career to boot. "Hi," she answered to the greeting.

"How are you?" the gentleman asked. ('Gentleman' my ass.)

"I'm fine and u?"

Steve inquired, "Is that you in the photo?"

"Yup, just me."

"Nice."

"Thank you. What do you look like?" I asked.

Steve gave the stats of 6'2" with dark hair and green eyes. Hmm, guess he grew an inch since we chatted last year or else must have been that his peacock feathers were fluffed out from the attractive blonde. "What do you do?" he asked.

"PR public relations," I answered.

"With a company?"

"No, representative, I have a partner . . . hang on telephone." I needed to take a break and catch my breath. I had Steve in a death grip by the balls for a change and this was going to be fun. Luckily I had the foresight to create an email address for this new nickname of Connie and sure enough he asked for the address while wishing to proceed to the more intimate area of instant messenger.

Hot damn this was great! I was playing him and he didn't seem to have a clue. Oh, there were a couple of slipups over several days with things semi-specific to me, Lisa. For example: to laugh out loud was usually typed 'lol' but on occasion I use all caps 'LOL' and Steve stopped to inquire as to my choice of all caps. My quick response was that the line was extremely funny.

The second slipup happened during the creation of a scenario with a guy and a girl. Example: he and she went to the beach. Lisa would say the man and the woman went to the beach. Steve stopped to make inquiry for the choice of pronouns. I am afraid that slip was a little more serious in pinpointing my personality. If Steve knew that it was me then he played along really well without revealing our little secret.

We communicated quite heavily now almost daily at times unless his workload was great or he had court. This man chatted differently with Connie though. He gave the woman more respect as a person then he did with me. For a change I enjoyed the camaraderie of his basic nature without all the piggy responses. The web cam was no longer a distraction as we enjoyed one another's company by verbal response only, creativity in just talking. At the time I didn't really think about this respect angle. The sad fact only hit me at a later date.

Each day our conversations began with a certain question, "What are you wearing?" My answers were elaborate business attire, power suits, stilettos, designer dresses and such. I was impressed with the creativity and he seemed impressed by the varied designs. In hindsight maybe he was waiting for names of couture designers but I'm only a country girl without knowledge of such things. Not that I don't wish for a mentor to teach me about famous fashion, but then again what would one do with knowledge of high style that I'll never be able to afford.

Occasionally Connie wore jeans on Friday or inappropriate sexy skirts and sweaters to which Steve questioned propriety. Connie just smiled and flirted in return which is what the lawyer desired in the long run.

Although this woman lived the life of a single gal she did have a live-in boyfriend that remained out of town a large percentage of time, but Connie remained faithful to him. With this small detail I imagine that Steve felt safe against the pressure of meeting someone. And if he realized it was me, Lisa, then we felt safe against any ridiculous pressure to pursue the naughty quest of meeting.

Late Friday afternoon came around one day and I stated that some co-workers were going out for drinks.

"Do you flirt?" he asked.

"Flirt?"

"Are you hit on by guys?"

"Yes, but I just shoot them down."

"You don't like attention?"

"It's no big deal. I don't need it but there is one guy though."

"Please tell."

I had Steve in my sights now. Let's just see how well he responds. "Yes, Pierce is younger than me. He works at the Robert Young Federal Building. I don't remember what he does. Its legal services or something." I had grabbed the St. Louis visitors guide and found this reference that any lawyer could trace. Sure enough Steve responded with 'be right back'. I don't know positively that he checked validity of the federal building but I like to think that he did.

Steve returned shortly. "Are you attracted to him?"

"He is very handsome, just too young for me. He has a crush on me though."

"You could have fun manipulating the situation." Well spoken by a lawyer that enjoys the rough sport of coercion.

I imagine Steve meant that I could manipulate Pierce's lust over Connie. Oh the tangled webs that we weave. Here I am in the throes of playing Steve while talking about playing someone that did not exist. *Laughing my ass off* But doggone it! I kept it all straight! I was an actress in a play while a writer creating a scenario at the same time. Help! Does this mean I use both sides of my brain at the same time? Probably not. Digressing and deviating of which I do very well.

Damn though, I started to think this would make one heck of a story, Steve and Connie, two attractive people—edgy, hard nosed individuals living daily power plays through their careers. Yup, I had another story to start. And write I did, very quickly in fact as I pumped out three pages in one day and then the next seven not too long after that. Ray asked for a part in this story of which I gave him Connie's partner in the public relation firm. The story is not complete as of yet but it is still seriously on the backburner, notes are strewn everywhere and my head is seriously clouded with many details that need to escape into a word document.

You know if Steve's path crossing my path holds any meaning at all it lies with this motivation that he's provided. He has been verbally thanked more than once for inspiration given by his online character, for those edgy provoking one-liners that simply drive me crazy leaving no direction but to create this over blown stuff. It fluffs his ego, as well as it should, to imagine that he can influence a woman the way that he does. Stand tall, Steve, and smile.

And Ray? He knows all about this obsessive fascination that I have with Steve. Of course he doesn't care for it one bit since we are boyfriend and girlfriend, nonetheless he puts up with the nonsense knowing my hardheaded fixation for challenge.

In the long run Ray proofed the writing of this new story, "Damn girl, you can write," he said making me feel very proud, and then he passed around my writing to some of his co-workers but, alas, men are not really into tantalizing romantic stories as we found out.

It was not a tale that could be read by my in-laws or anyone in this community as they only read inspirational novels and scripture, however I was not asking anyone from around here to read my works. Except, if only Steve would read this new story . . .

I am completely embarrassed to make admittance of the fact that I sent the story to three or four New York attorneys with Steve's first name, same month and year of birth. Of course I received no replies, or even from the man that had been a professor of writing from a certain university out west. So I am not sure whether Steve received the story sample or not. I desperately needed to get it to him. Although providing him with the material only meant that this little secret would be given away. He would eventually find out that Connie was actually me, Lisa, and the game would be over. Options were carefully weighed whether I actually wanted to give the secret away or not. The truth is always found out one way or another, comes to the surface, so what the heck.

One afternoon he and I entered instant messenger to chat. I pretended to remain busy with serious work and then suddenly asked him out of the blue. "Would you like to see what I am working on? I can send the job order through instant messenger."

"Sure." He received the file but said nothing.

"Did you read it yet?" I inquired.

"Should I?"

"Only if you have time. It's no big deal." Oh, but it was a big deal, a very big deal.

A little time past. "Who is this?"

"It's me Lisa." I'm not sure if he remembered who Lisa was and so I stated my primary nickname.

"Who?" He inquired.

"It's me!"

Steve had me frantically grasping for straws strewn across the keyboard and I am certain he could feel my nervous tension through the screen as I revealed my true identity. My heart was pounding. "Let's see," he asked while wishing for me to turn the web cam on.

I turned on the blasted device so that we would stop playing the game of 'who is this'. I felt that I had played Steve extremely hard now, fooling him completely and so I asked out of true concern. "Are you ok?"

"Sure, why wouldn't I be?"

"Just wondering because I fooled you." Paybacks are hell as Steve fooled me first on more than one occasion.

"Do you like fooling people?"

"I just got you back for those other times."

"Take your shirt off."

"No."

"Just do it!"

Damn him and damn the web cam! His name was quickly blocked before shutting down the computer.

Sitting quietly in the chair staring into oblivious space I suddenly realized a harsh reality. Steve had not been as rude to Connie as he is to me. Perhaps it's the fact that she was a career woman and of a higher standing than me. It is depressing to think that I never became the complete woman that I wished to be. I wanted to be Connie with the productive career and power suits and enjoy Friday evenings out on the town with co-workers . . . not this plain Midwestern wife with a husband that has forgotten how to nurture his home life.

A few hours later I came back to the computer and deleted Steve's name from Connie's and Lisa's instant messengers. I was finished with Steve again. If he wanted to chat he could find my nickname in the chat room some other morning. The lawyer would now be out of my life for over six months.

This certain winter many things were going on within my marriage. There were many other changes that began to tug at our lives. My husband began suffering from scary bouts of sleep apnea. He would wake up in the night unable to catch his breath in a very frightening process. Standing next to the bed he panicked while stomping his foot on the floor, fist pounding his chest trying to open the airways. The air passages just suddenly close up but when he is upright they quickly open again. He is a heavy snorer of which I refer to as the 'chain saw snore' if that is any excuse. Also his body shape is that of a football player with a thick neckline and he never had his tonsils or anodes removed as a child.

We did see a doctor about the sleep apnea and went through the process of a sleep test but the uncomfortable tests were inconclusive. I do question the small town doctor's ability and wonder if another professional might be more thorough. However the tests are expensive and not covered by insurance so I doubt we will ever go through that again.

With regular nightly disturbances we both felt that neither one was getting a good night's sleep so I began spending many nights on the couch. By February I had a single daybed in the computer room that subsequently became my primary sleeping quarters, and still is to this day. My husband and I felt strange resorting to this drastic measure but it did help our situation. We both began sleeping better and thankfully his sleep apnea subsided.

For awhile I joined him first thing in the evening so that we could talk about the day's events or make plans for tomorrow, or I would rub my feet over his so that we could each relax and begin to fall asleep easily. It was a longtime ritual that we started early on in the marriage and created the reference of 'we were surely made for each other'. But sex was really beginning to fade with implementation of the second bed. What used to be a once a week ritual now seemed to be every other week or less. He is always tired and I am tired of trying to activate him. Well, we are in our mid-forties if that's any excuse.

I truly believe that my husband is also aging fast. His memory slips ferociously, his driving scares me and his thought processes are so slow. He subsequently gets mad at himself for not concentrating on facts at hand or forgetting things in mid search. Of course he is completely geared to sports, sport scores and sports trivia which are always on the forefront of his mind. He can recite baseball, basketball or football trivia along with scores over a span of 30 years or more, but has no clue as to the workings of matters such as insurance, the stock market, IRA's or things of a financial standing. It is quite frightening to say the least. I am a little savvier but not much.

My husband doesn't even wish to learn about these important financial necessities of life which is becoming an embarrassment when discussing these matters with one who does understand their workings. We ignore the problem, don't do anything about it and hope it just goes away. Of course this is the wrong approach. Doctors could possibly help his slowing processes, or a good therapist.

There's also another instance pertaining to his slowing processes. It was a simple correction in the checkbook. Let's see if it can be explained correctly. I had finished writing a check with the last check number of 1000. We continued to use the debit card as usual over the next few days. And then one day he repeated the 1000 check number again, writing it in the book. We noticed there was a problem a page later but could not figure out the culprit. I called the bank asking for the missing amount. Well, to make a long story short I figured out what was wrong and began physically jumping up and down "It's not my fault! I didn't do it so don't blame me." Yes, we enjoy gloating when we are right.

After a complete explanation he still did not understand that he had repeated the same check number. Suddenly I look out the kitchen window and the wind is blowing trash across the patio after the cat had already made a stinky mess in the laundry room that screamed for attention. I'm yelling, "Can't you figure it out? I've got to pick up garbage from the yard before it blows into the crabby neighbor's lawn and the cat needs cleaning up after." Not to mention the ten other items I am multitasking on a busy morning. "Just scribble 1 over the last 0 and fix the next four check numbers."

"But now what a minute and listen to me . . ."

I walked away. He finally figured out the problem on his own and fixed it.

Quickly, I must also recall his inquiry of the county seat's zip code. I relayed the easy number and then he asked how to make out an envelope. "Does the zip code go in front of the . . . umm, town and umm, state?" Has he never looked at a piece of mail? I know he has addressed envelopes before. My mother was even astounded with the strange revelation. His mother would simply freak. These are only two scenes of many simplistic, naïve situations of which withstand basic mental reasoning. But do I have to explain everything? Alright fine, blame me for failing to have any patience. I give in, give up and retire to the land of fairytales.

# CHAPTER 6

Wonderful springtime arrived with great fanfare as always while colorful daffodils, tulips and crocuses bloomed and leaves sprouted on trees. Springtime is like an effervescent tonic leaving me bouncing off walls with the high energy of youthful inspiration. Landscaping calls to me for a round of exploration to discover every tiny green sprout on every plant and shrub. What would be better than to top it all off with an exuberant trip to New York to see my boyfriend? One more lie was managed from the big bag of tricks with reference to the bi-curious girl that I allegedly spent long weekends with. Hubby bought it again. Obviously he still wished to meet this person and spend time with us but I came up with yet another excuse just the same.

I told him, "Maybe sometime this summer, that is if she can get away from this new boyfriend that takes up so much of her time. We'll just have to wait and see." There, maybe if the bi-curious girl was too busy for us that would hold my husband at bay.

Flying into New York on a Friday afternoon in the warm month of May was so much more pleasant than the wintertime had been, plus the fiasco of being stranded at the Philly airport. We made our sappy scene in the terminal after I stepped through the security doors and then drove a rental car to the little cabin in the woods. Routines are never changed as usual and we dove into bed first.

This trip provided two full days of blissful togetherness. We drove up to Kingston to visit with his family and friends on one of those days. Ray also took me to a bend of the Hudson River to observe how wide the river actually is. It reminds me of the Mississippi River at certain points, a grandiose splendor indeed, and such history to boot.

The impressive view contains different elements of nature surrounding a sandy beach park. Shuffling across the dirty sand we collected a souvenir of a black barbed seed pod that fell from a tree. Ray stated that as a kid he stepped on one of these and it hurt like hell when the long barb went into his foot. Neither one of us knows the name of the tree that this came from but the pod now sits on my computer desk. The seeds still rattle inside of the strange shaped pod. Maybe I should plant them to find out what kind of tree it produces.

Another souvenir collected is pieces of washed up brick from an old brick factory that has long since retired. Pieces of the orange-red brick now reside near my goldfish pond along the gravel walkway. When the fish are fed I see the bright objects and remember my special time at the edge of the Hudson River with Ray.

While experiencing all of natures wonders at the river's edge my cell phone suddenly rang. It was my husband.

"Hi. What are you doing?"

Think fast, think fast. "Oh not much. I'm just sitting outside right now."

"Isn't it raining down there too?"

Oh no, it was raining back home in the Midwest. I had forgotten about flying out of rain clouds yesterday morning. New York was blessed with mostly sunny skies as well as screaming seagulls! I had to get off this phone and fast. "Oh it stopped raining here but yeah, the skies are still cloudy."

Ray had walked away to give some privacy. I turned to him and shrugged my shoulders and pointed to the screaming seagulls. He rolled his eyes while not quite understanding my predicament.

My husband replied quite naïve to the dilemma, "Ahh I see. Are you having a good time?"

"Uh huh, we went shopping for groceries yesterday. Last night we watched a little TV after fixing spaghetti and tonight we plan on fixing Italian breaded pork chops." I listened while he took time explaining his night and plans for the afternoon and evening. The seagulls failed to give reprieve as I tried shielding the phone's mouth piece a little bit. For some reason I was nervous and unable to focus on what he was saying. It was like he had interrupted my perfect world of contentment and discovery of the Hudson River here in New York State.

I made some excuse about needing to go soon and he just replied, "You seem to have all sorts of time for your friends but you can't spend some time talking to me?"

"No, no, no that's not what I'm saying. I just need to get a move on. We're getting ready to go into town again. We forgot to get something at the grocery store for tonight."

"Oh I see."

We said our goodbyes normally and everything was fine but my nerves were shot for awhile. That scared me. It was just too close for comfort. Thank goodness he never called while I was waiting at an airport. Screaming intercom systems along with flight schedules would be a dead give away. It seems mighty inevitable that one of these days we're going to get caught and then there's going to be hell to pay, but for some weird reason I don't care about getting caught . . . or by whom. Freedom could only be a thankful release from shackling bonds.

My sister knew of these escapades from just about the beginning through long conversations about my boyfriends beginning with Ben. She was aware of the necklace that Ben had sent the previous year and all the while sis observed physical changes that were beginning to happen. Behavior changes happened across the board. She witnessed my sense of freedom, the freedom of knowing who one is. Life is to be lived to the fullest. It is a precious gift to be enjoyed. There was love and romance in my heart again. A deep sense of sensuality drove my inner essence whether derived from my boyfriends or whether it was sensuality derived from basically loving life itself. Who is to say? Optimism is a cherished gift that prolongs life, keeps one youthful.

Other physical changes consisted from a different hairstyle to a sparkle in my eyes or the provocative grin that held many deep secrets. My sister witnessed transformations including the weight loss, building of muscle tone due to lifting weights and purchasing a new style of clothes. I was no longer the same person inside or out and it showed.

You know those photos that sis and I took that one Valentine's Day? A year later that girl is long gone. The person in the photos was a frumpy little housewife with an 80's hairstyle. The girl was a little over weight and void of muscle tone or definition. And the poor girl's smile . . . oh my . . . she was so backward and repressed. Even Ray agrees that those photos are no longer me although he still thinks they are provocative.

I am contemplating whether to tell the reader one more dark secret. If this story is to help the reader understand this total being then I must reveal everything. At the same time hoping that someday someone may be helped by my revelations. We must all realize that things in life are not nearly as bad as they may seem, unless one is physically abused or in dire circumstances of suffering then we are most likely able to get through this basic existence.

After losing that last job and falling into a deep depression. Not only thoughts of ending it all had crossed my mind. In fact that mere instance of ending it all was realistically only a cry for help. I would not have blown my brains out behind the rotting tree. Although at the same time there was so much negativity building toward this Midwestern community, as well as the fact that I could no longer hold down a job. This secluded county is so depressed from job closings and in dire need of economic development. Yes, depressed economic development is everywhere and vastly proven in government statistics.

And then there is this religious sect that only attends school to the 8th grade. Mentality around this sectarian community fails to see much into the realm of sciences, politics or anything of an extreme nature. I cannot quite explain this feeling of such prejudice aimed at me. Perhaps it is a couple of sisters-in-law that cause a bit of narrow mindedness due to clash of personalities. But by God, I am no less of a person because our choice was to not have children. How narrow minded, idiotic and estrogen induced for women to think that way, to imagine all women as baby makers.

There is one woman that is very estrogen induced and has babysat all of her life, children being the next best thing to . . . leading into meaningful conversation laced with baby words. She cannot wait to become a grandmother which is all fine and understandable but not the choice for every woman. It was during this past Christmas Day at the in-laws when she found her way to sit next to me. Watching me I suppose. She simply finds a way to observe whatever it is I'm doing or butts into conversations that are none of her business, stating that she knows how I feel and what I am thinking. No mild mannered woman knows what I am thinking or how I feel, please give me a break. Possibly she is wishing to be a mother figure since she is a year older, but . . . all expletives deleted, I sure as heck don't need another mother figure. One per person is just fine thank you very much.

Sitting side by side this woman gathered two small toddler's close as I watched in amazement as she put her face within inches of theirs, somehow this seemed like a motherly example for those less estrogen induced. Slowly with her soft gentle hands she brought the toddler's heads together while saying something about 'the little baby's lips kissing'. Delicately pressing their small heads together the children did not want to kiss while looking terrified and confused but she became all consumed by their precious little lips puckering in the frame of a smooch. Good Lord, give me a fast car and a man with fortitude and rock music blaring through the car's speakers! The little baby's lips? *Shaking my head* We are two of a kind.

Now to get back on track again, explaining my past working experience at this time of the depression I had closed down the third print shop. Twenty years had been devoted to a career in Printing Technology but computers took over my job as the middle man in pre-press. Many people can understand the dilemma of loosing ones job due to layoffs or the equivalent. The circumstance is quite an upheaval to the whole family, emotionally as well as financially.

The second owner of the first print shop, where I had been employed for 13 years, went to prison for money laundering, quite an embarrassing situation for the previous owner that was a good family man. One fateful morning all the employees walked out leaving the criminal to flounder and fall helplessly into the hands of the law. Good riddance to him.

The second print shop was run by a man with a severe bi-polar disorder. There were holes in the walls where he had punched a fist through, and at times one could hear through an office door as he shook the filing cabinet while growling foul obscenities. The darkroom equipment was cheap and in serious disrepair, the shoddy equipment would no longer recalibrate for proper film development. And this ill tempered boss ran off employees by the scores including me after he ripped the pre-press phone from the wall.

At the third print shop I tried working from the front desk placing customer's orders but unfortunately it closed its doors due to lack of business. It didn't matter. I was doing a miserable job while out of my element of the darkroom and preferring physical labor. I felt like such a failure. Job hopping was beginning to create an ugly resume. And of course there is also the two interesting years that I spent with the drug runners at the trucking company which is an unbelievable book unto itself. The company is now closed as well due to unorganized management.

I was now out of work and with no skills to proceed into a different career. My husband said no to the idea of college but college might have been a productive venture for me. I could have branched out while meeting new people with like minds and enjoyed a new type of livelihood. The reader has already observed how many inspired interests swim through this creative mind. Perhaps I could meet professors or people with an advanced way of thinking and we could put our minds together and create a better mouse trap, or change the eco system, find a way to feed the starving. Simply over time I would enjoy attending parties with like minded people, communicating, laughing, and trying new foods from a different culture. This dreamy mind is so repressed within these stagnant four walls.

And so in this revelation that I am trying to state it is with embarrassment although one might find it power for the course, or nonchalant in basic simplicity. But I told my sister that if anything happened, maybe even divorce, I would be out of this community in an instant. I could walk away from this community without even a discerning glance in the rearview mirror. She questioned, "What about your family? You can't walk away from us because I need you." It's true my sister needs my nearby presence desperately. She is weaker than me and will admit it.

"I'm sorry but yes. I could easily just walk away from it all. I am done. I'm finished with this area. I quit. There is no more trying to fit in."

"Do you really think you can leave your family behind that easily?"

"Yup." The quick response was not meant to be cruel or to push her away in any way shape or form and she understands this fact. "I would like to find a little cottage on a beach in the Carolinas or East Coast and maybe meet some nice gentleman with children or grandchildren and watch them grow up. We would attend their plays and ballgames and be a real family. On weekends we would encourage the grandchildren to come over while enjoying cookouts or go swimming. Just listen to them as they explain everything important in their little lives." I painted the picture with broad strokes of the pen just for her. "And then you and mom could come to the east coast for a vacation to see me."

"Well I can see that happening. It doesn't take much of an excuse to get Mom out of the house."

"I'll never have that dream here. All I ever wanted to do was live happily ever after with someone who cares." And sis knows that if I had kids I would want a girl to raise. Funny thing is Ray has two daughters, cute girlie girls that enjoy communicating. Forgive me but my husbands nieces are cold not open. They have the look of sheep led to slaughter except for a couple of cute girls that are going to college. Bless her hearts.

But unfortunately my life is not set up for children. Not this way. Believe me if there were children in this household they would be raised properly. There would be no porn on the television. Their time on the computer would be strictly monitored as would be mine also. They would be allowed the right to behave as a child, to laugh and speak their minds. And I would talk until blue in the face about how drugs are bad and sex is only for when you are old enough to love someone very much. Also, whatever you do don't ruin your scholarship chances because your potential in the real world depends totally on this ability to attend college. Study hard because your future is everything. Sis knows I would be a good parent and so does her teenager that I care about. Such is life.

How many other women suffer this same fantasy? How many wish for the sober vision of leaving it all behind and moving on with a new way of life? Of course a new way of life does not always mean a better way of living, along with the false premise that ending a marriage will bring a better turn of events for a new tomorrow. Falling into the trap of that falsehood is dangerous, very dangerous. Life throws difficult challenges while we are content and when we are not. Life throws a curve ball when we are happy beside a man or when we are not. Having a man in your life does not make a woman whole. It helps to have a congenial partner by your side but it's not the bottom line. Finances, security and safety are most important, as well as one's health.

Of course these are only my opinions but I believe these theories to be on track. There are so many marriages that are capable of succeeding if both parties would just try to make them work. Too many people remark that they have irreconcilable differences and leave the marriage floundering with those very words. What a bunch of bunk and a blatant cop out. Sure, I suffered through the first marriage and bailed after he bailed but we were both too young. He walked out our home into another girl's arms. Oh that hurt like hell! I cried a river for weeks on end. But you know what? If we had gotten counseling we could have worked things out. Unfortunately some young men are not into counseling. They run like crazy in the other direction while taunting concerned parents (and his priest) in the frantic escape 'you'll never find me so leave me alone'.

Ray is aware of my desire to leave this community without ever looking back. He knows me very well but is unable to offer this substantial living that I have right now. We are in complete agreement that it would be foolish for me to give up financial and retirement security. Through embarrassment of this simple revelation of wishing to leave this community I am afraid should anyone from this area become privileged with this information they would swiftly throw open the gates wide. 'Go if you so desire to be free!' But I can't leave. I need the security of this home and of its four confining walls.

June has always been a bad month for some strange reason. Perhaps astrological speaking as it is three months before my birthday while at an angle of troubles and secrets. My first marriage was in the month of June. There are other instances of bad luck in the workforce during the month of June. Also, I seem to have gotten in trouble with my in-laws around Memorial Day for several years in a row. They have a big garden and I don't come around to help. Yeah, well, I get myself into trouble there. The excuse to my husband is that I was not raised around a big garden. Must I be condemned for not being a slave to another's tradition? My parents went to the grocery store for all of our food. Except tomatoes which Dad grew in the summer and yes, to this day I grow tomatoes as well. Oh and hey! Last year my tomatoes were better than the in-laws. Mine didn't get mushy and I purchased our plants from Wal-Mart instead of the Amish. Alright, zip it on the gloating babe. Deviating and digressing again. (One last note though concerning fertilized tomatoes: their luck was most likely derived from the fact that I watered most mornings with pond water that is high in nitrogen and minerals from fish by-products and algae. Gardeners take note: this truly is beneficial in addition to regular fertilizing.)

Concerning bad luck in the month of June—playing around on the computer one day I finally found the name of the swingers club for my husband. Yup, it was the exact same name that his best buddy's new wife had explained. This woman told us that her best friend had attended the club with another couple a few years back. So my husband and I checked out the web site together that evening and then he abruptly asked, "Want to go once?"

"I don't know. This is pretty far out."

While at the computer we checked out prices and procedure for gaining access to the club. The post mentioned strict importance of communicating to your spouse over how to approach many sexual scenarios, or what to do if you met someone that you know personally and how to avoid embarrassment. Listed were also questions pertaining to many issues: Are you in this for yourselves only? Are you interested in meeting others? Do you wish to attract the attention of a third person for a threesome, or perhaps to meet another couple to engage in a foursome? Local hotels were also listed on the site for slipping into private liaisons. How convenient and well thought out.

We sent an email to the club and waited for the call which 'would happen shortly' the post read.

Sitting in the living room together that evening with the television blaring we waited. Communication flowed rapidly between us in anticipation of the phone call as I asked, "Well, how should we approach this? You know I want to experience another man while I'm still in my prime. I told you that last year while chatting with Ben. It doesn't bother me to see you with a stripper so it wouldn't bother me if you engaged in sex with another woman. But would it upset you seeing me have sex with another man?"

Should the reader ask why it would not faze me seeing my husband having sex with another woman, implication of the answer scares me. Maybe I'm not ready to respond to that question just yet. However should an inquiring mind press with allegation that my love for the man has slipped. The inquiring mind should be considered quite perceptive.

He answered my previous question of watching me have sex with another man. "That's a tough one. I don't know. If that's what you want sure, as long as I can be with someone too. But whatever we do it has to be together." He firmly stipulated this rule for any sexual exchange.

"So you're saying a foursome?"

"Yeah, that or a threesome with another girl."

The phone finally rang and it was a woman with a girlish southern voice. It was a pleasant voice that became very helpful. Before we knew it we had a date for this coming Saturday night at the swinger club. My husband was obviously excited as its right up his alley, something to take porn addiction to a new level. One might add ascending to a new level where he could actually act out a fantasy or receive sexual pleasure from the female sex.

At the time, yes, I was excited of exploration also. There was a little something in the back of my mind that still wanted to flirt with a man, the perfect all American guy. But in hindsight I forgot to be nervous of mingling with strangers in a lounge type atmosphere. I am not such a people person. Remember as a shy individual I hate people. (Irish blarney) Perhaps its time that this silly holdover from my youth needs to be released.

Years ago while in our 20's we went out on the town every Saturday evening to night clubs, drinking hotspots and lounges. I struggled to have a good time but knowing it was the thing to do I suffered through the age related ritual. Young people need to get out and socialize. Sure, sitting at home is also boring and certainly no way to catch a man.

This agreement to attend the swinger club was mostly because of my husband though. It was his desire. Who am I to deprive him of sexual exploration? Ray was my fantasy of which I had delved into with reckless abandon. What's good for the gander is power for the goose, or vice versa.

Saturday evening the dark neighborhood was seedy looking with ancient brick buildings and a run down area of worn out houses. The oddly shaped parking lot was not very large for the building's size and we parked on the broken up concrete early in the evening when there were no more than five vehicles at the joint.

Greeting us from a narrow foyer was the woman with the southern accent. She was a pretty gal with blue eyes and long blonde hair pulled up in cascading tendrils. My husband filled out the necessary paperwork before we received our membership card and temporary admittance. Members are permanent, but dues are on a basis of one month, six months or a year. Diane (her husband was owner of the club) then finished the lengthy paperwork along with rules before taking us on a hasty tour of the building.

Large red double doors suddenly opened into a dark lounge. Temperature of the room was cool from air conditioning while red hot streamers hung from tall open beams of the old building. I sensed that we were delving into a strange netherworld. Diane quickly walked straight ahead with us in trail. We past several small tables with red table cloths adorned with lit hurricane lamps. My eyes fell to the long but narrow dance floor which was lit from above with colorful tract lighting. A disco ball also hung from the center of this space over the wooden floor.

"This is the dance cage," Diane began. "Only one person is allowed in the cage at a time. Clothing is optional. You may see some nudity here but there is absolutely no sex allowed in the cage." She then rapidly moved on.

My eyes then fell to the stripper poles—two to be exact side by side with mirrors on two walls of the corner. Diane then quickly walked down the isle and past two groups of people. In hind sight I should have noticed these two groups of people. One group would soon become our future as they watched Diane take this new couple on the tour. The newbie's are always succulent bait for the cause.

"My husband is the disk jockey right now. We're supposed to have someone take over pretty soon. And then here are the restrooms." She continued her brisk walk in a floppy dress and tall platform heels as her wide hips swayed. "This is the bar. All soft drinks are free. You just need to bring your own alcohol."

We rounded a corner into another room where sight of pool tables and a food display opened up. "We always have sandwiches and relish trays for everybody. A night of socializing can cause a big appetite." I noticed a colorful tray of chocolate covered strawberries and knew I would be back to delve into those later.

Sounds suddenly seemed to soften in a corner of the building as I noticed two plain doors. One was a black exit door and the other Diane began to open. My husband and I were all eyes now as we entered the secret domain of sex clubs. The first lounge was large, open and comfortable with two big couches and a large square coffee table. Lighting was dim with one small lamp and an electric fireplace towering against one wall.

But the hostess did not slow her brisk pace. She described each room quickly as we passed, "This is the blue room . . . the harem room . . . room of stars." It was painted dark blue with glow in the dark stars affixed all around. There were no doors on any of the entries only a thin black veil of sheer cloth and beads to walk through which created absolutely no privacy. Diane said, "Each room has a small lamp that is to be left on at all times. If you come back here we ask that you don't stand and stare into the rooms."

We strolled past a bright room across from two small restrooms. This one caught our eye as it was large with two white couches . . . and a sex swing hanging from the ceiling. I had only heard of those or maybe saw a picture of one once. Oh, I remember now. It was in bathroom of two famous people, from the sex tape that they had made. One could imagine that the swing might cause some interesting sex. It seems as though the device would take all physical pressure off both the man and woman while producing some pure pounding pleasure. My interest remains perked to this day.

Our hostess had one last instruction. "If you are back here and the overhead lighting comes on you need to immediately get dressed. The police have a right to come back here at any time. Also when you leave this area you have to leave in pairs. We ask that you leave with the same person you came back here with."

My husband and I slowly returned to the table. I'm not sure what I was thinking at this point in time. Maybe chocolate covered strawberries were still on my mind but my husband's eyes were wide open as he enjoyed himself immensely, and maybe I was engulfed in watching the two women across the room devouring one another in a lip lock while their husbands played pool.

We quickly met another couple who were part of the welcoming committee. They were younger and made us feel welcomed as the clubs essence was explained. The wife remarked that she had reservations about the lifestyle from the beginning and offered a motto of just don't do anything that doesn't feel comfortable. She explained that most people only come here to socialize in an adult atmosphere, meaning that they are only here to add a little spice to their sex lives. That made excellent sense.

Both the husband and his wife seemed so honest, open and down to earth, and not highly sexual in the least. I just couldn't see them engulfed in this way of life. As the evening wore on I also failed to see where the owners could be involved as swingers either. They were into only each other as I watched them hug and provide support. Perhaps it's only business to the owners or maybe they are more private in their hedonistic exchange with other couples. One can't blame them if that is the case, privacy factor being a major issue.

That evening at the club my husband and I were all eyes as we watched people and the dance floor. This is difficult to write as I am still dealing with unsettled issues from our recent past but this particular night was an attempt to please my husband. While sitting at the table my husband was busy getting an eyeful of seminude women placing their bodies on display while I quietly sat there enveloped in my backward nature. Part of me wished to publicly reveal my prowess as a woman but public displays of sexuality just is not my character.

Halfway through the evening another couple approached us. They were an attractive pair very nice and quite articulate. They stated that they had been watching us from across the room and wished for us to join their party. Well, we had been watching the wife on the dance floor through several songs. She was not the best dancer but she was extremely confident in displaying her sexuality and also had abs to die for. This cute woman was not tall by any means but for her age she had a body that was tight and awesomely structured, not an ounce of fat anywhere. I'm not even sure if the poor woman could have been a double A bra size.

They were sitting with another couple that had approached us earlier in the evening. We agreed to sit with them and walking up to their table things suddenly seemed like a set up in the way chairs were configured. I was situated between the two men and my husband sat between the two women. Dialog instantly became fast and furious from talkative personalities under the influence of alcohol. Over and over words were repeated with loud reference to the fact that one can make as much as they want out of the swinger lifestyle. Just take it only as far as you want to take it.

"What are you guys into? Do you like to swing or just in it for yourselves?" Someone asked.

My husband spoke first. "We're new at this but we probably would be into a threesome with another girl most likely. My wife has been with another girl." He stated confidently with a smile.

Oh crap! Sorry ladies but I have not. Her real name is Ray. Oh gee! I wished that he would have kept his mouth shut but there was no turning back. In reality these two women could probably see that I was not putting myself out for their response.

All the while the older gentleman began placing his hands all over my body. What was I to do?! It was a swingers club for Pete's sake. Was I to say 'get your bloody hands off me you loathsome creep'? The attention I received was quite confusing while the two men inquired what I wanted from the lifestyle.

Playing everyone's game I replied, "Well I suppose a threesome or foursome is what would interest us the most. I'm really new at this and don't know how my husband would respond. I don't know if he would be upset to see me with another man."

The older man quickly pointed out that my husband and his wife were face to face and talking close into one another's ear. "He doesn't seem to mind."

Good point but this was just plain weird. I was still not certain of my husband's reaction should I eventually become engaged in sex with another man. As was stated before I did not care if he had sex with another woman. The mere act would only validate my affair with Ray. And besides, what the heck were we talking about sex anyway? I was not going to have sex with anyone tonight.

I quickly told the older man that I had just returned from New York after seeing my boyfriend and that my husband does not know about this. Perhaps I told him the secret in hopes that he would see my interests were elsewhere or that I had issues and certainly did not need anymore. The ploy failed to work. Ray has tried informing me that when telling another man about a boyfriend that only turns them onto the fact that they might have a chance at being another boyfriend. He is right. I've seen this happen over and over now.

"Come on, let's go dance," the older gentleman requested. He was probably about five years older than me with grey hair and glasses. He was not unattractive and was a good height while dressed quite nicely as well. We went to the dance floor and so did my husband and his wife.

Let's call them Adam and Eve for lack of better names. Adam was unlike my husband as his muscle tone was soft. I will say that my husband's rock hard muscles, gluts and fists of iron are very nice. But Adam was soft and gentle . . . and could dirty dance with the best of them. So that's why the man's leg is between the women's legs. So that he can raise his thigh and press against her clit for arousal. Wow! And oh my!

Wouldn't you know it the next song was a slow dance. During the second slow dance the other gentleman from our party broke in. He was a tall man and not the best looking as well as a big talker. His bad breath was atrocious and I quickly tired of his incessant mindless chatter while wishing for a change of venue, but endured this unwelcome development to the end. After the song was over he suddenly kissed me deeply with tongue. Oh, how awful. In the outside world I would not have given this man any basic time of day. I was slowly being eaten alive by two die hard hedonists. And yes, someone had been to and explained the fine Hedonism resort in the Caribbean, a place where hands roam freely over anyone and everyone, a large continuous orgy of nude and copulating pleasure. Again this is not me. One on one is quite enough thank you very much.

So why did I stay and endure this revolting situation? I owed my husband his jollies due to my brazen affair. Pity my husband couldn't just find sexual satisfaction with some stripper. Kinda sick that I have to help him find another woman to have sex with. Why can't he just accomplish this task on his own?

This hell hole of a cave grew deeper as we were lured to the cavern of pleasure-seeking delights . . . the sex rooms in the back of the building. We calmly strolled to the back rooms along with the two other couples, intent only to view the pleasure of others so the statement was made by someone. All the while sounds of sex could be heard and seen through open doors. One could easily view the nakedness and observe aroused men on top while thrusting into a woman. It seems like hedonistic hands roamed over my curves as I glanced into another's act of sexuality.

In a solitary back corner was a small room with a solid door, sound proof so one of women said. The two women went in and one lay back on the couch, her panties were removed and her legs spread. Before anyone knew what was happening the women were hungrily at each other. The older gentleman turned to me and remarked with a smile, "Eve said that she's been craving pussy all day."

My husband certainly got an eyeful. "This is one my fantasy's come true," he said, "seeing two women together."

One could not help but watch their arousal; hear their arousal as Eve buried her face causing shear ecstasy to the girl. Within moments Eve got up and lay on the couch with panties gone and legs spread as the other women returned the favor. I could only think of my husband telling these people that I had been with a woman. I had not and had absolutely no desire to join them. Oh, these people had to know, they had to see right through me with the fact that I stood there like a dummy.

My shame is prevalent with the underground mentality of this seedy business and knowing what I must reveal. Remember it's all in the process of coming to a conclusion of knowing who I am by what has been done. There are times when I can weather shame by throwing caution to the wind but regrettably it returns to the fact that what others think does matter, to most of us anyway. Holding on to a little shame reminds of us of our teenage years when mean kids could reduce another child to nothingness with harsh comments. Why do we gauge ourselves by what others think or say? I'm sure several answers would be quite interesting to hear, the intellectual answers that is.

In the back room of the swinger club we three couples progressed over to a series of three couches in a U shape formation. Adam sat next to me. All I remember was glancing over to Eve as she sat with the tall man and her hand was down his pants causing him much pleasure, stroking the full length of his manhood as his eyes glazed over from sheer enjoyment. They were watching me perhaps while waiting for my reaction. I was startled to say the least. The man had stated that he wanted me but I wanted nothing to do with their situation. My eyesight fell to the ground disengaging from their act of intense pleasure. Adam's hands continued to roam over my body. I suppose the next thing I remember was that we began kissing. It was alright, not too startling at the time.

My husband was not attracted to the tall man's wife and so in time the third couple respectably got up to leave, politely stating their goodbyes. My husband was next to Eve once the four of us were left alone. Adam and I began kissing again until I heard Eve's moans of pleasure. I turned around and glanced over just at that moment to see that my husband was between her legs. It was surreal but I didn't care. Ray was my physical boyfriend. I had told my husband that I wished to sleep with another man while I was still young enough to feel confident about my body.

Boldly I tossed a leg over Adam straddling him to his delight. Granted we were still fully clothed. "Let me take off my glasses first," he stated. Grinding my pelvis against his full blown hardness biological facts took over as he asked, "Do you want to take off your pants?"

The moans of Eve and me filled the air with the men giving oral contact. Our sounds drove each other as well as our husbands. It's not known who came first and I don't know if we were being watched by outsiders but the loud sounds of explosion would have drawn any curious onlookers.

Our evening ended with an exchange of email addresses and the wish to meet at the club again in a couple of weeks. As we walked toward the door I felt as though we were in a dream and remember seeing three or four short, completely nude little nymphs with fleshy curves playing on the dance floor. It looked like a medieval painting come to life, quite strange to say the least.

Out in the car my husband and I were mostly smiles. I asked, "What did we just do?" He didn't respond with much if I recall correctly. The car pulled onto the highway and all I could repeat over and over was, "What did we just do?" Outside of town we settled into the long drive home. He was tired while my mind raced. Real answers were elusive at this late hour of the night. But one thing remained. Why did I let my husband pull me down to his level of porn? I went into this evening as an enabler but came out with a completely different set of circumstances. Then horrible resentment began to build toward him, toward Adam and toward that filthy place. He could not wait until we returned to hedonistic pleasures in a couple of weeks but I didn't want to be a piece of female meat landing in the hands of strange men. Ray, Brad and Steve were not strangers, I chose them. And besides Brad, Steve and I had not known actual physical touch. Lucky me. The very idea of another man was a complete turn off now, quite repugnant.

My husband had a taste (pardon the rude pun) of another world that he could revel in. Would he actually sell me out to any interested guy? Confusion set in. I agreed to go to the swinger club in the first place, wanting a man's attention of which I received. Was it not on my own terms? The move to continue the sexual exchange with Adam came from me. Possibly this was out of curiosity but you know if my husband had not been there I would not have gone through with the act. In fact I would not have even been in that building at all. I truly began to hate him. He was killing me from inside. If only some money would materialize or if Ray could come into more money I would divorce this porn addicted man and move to New York in an instant. Oh, how in the world was I going to tell this situation to Ray? I wanted to cry but couldn't, not in front of my husband. Not in front of the man that wanted to sell me to any bidder. Had I become a victim to men by mere fact that I enjoyed attention from the opposite sex? I was so confused and lost respect for all men. Chatting was the furthest thing from my mind now and I avoided it for several weeks. The very thing that I had wished for—attention from men had regretfully turned on me.

Alone in the single bed in my own room I tried to get to some sleep. It was difficult. I still wanted to cry but couldn't. This sickening strangle hold was tearing me apart. Tears were elusive . . . that is, until morning. Burying my face in the pillow they finally flowed freely as my body shook uncontrollably. This emotional state needed to be broken as I grabbed the cell phone to call Ray and revealed the story of our night at the swinger club. I revealed everything except the act of oral sex. He couldn't know that part. It would break his heart. I felt so ashamed and degraded.

"As long as nothing happened then you're alright," he spoke while trying to soothe with reassurance. I sobbed unable to speak. "Hun, I feel so sorry for you but I don't know what to do." He continued to try reassurance, "I know why you feel so bad. You were afraid to tell me because you thought that I'd be disappointed."

That was a different angle and no that's not what I thought previously. Well, it was now. Was he disappointed in me? Playing up the angle I stated, "I told that man that I wasn't interested in him because of you, because you are my boyfriend." It was true that I told Adam about my boyfriend in hopes that he would remove his hands from my body. Alas, it didn't work and most likely only accentuated his interest proving that this woman would stray.

"See, you were thinking about me. You were afraid of hurting me."

Oh God, I hated this situation that trapped me within its sick clutches. I was hurting Ray and my husband was hurting me. "He wants to go back to the club again. I can't bear to have that man's hands on me again. If I had some way to get out of this house I would be out of here in an instant. It's not right to live this way. It's stupid to live this way. And you know his family would be shocked if they found out about the strippers and the swinger club."

Ray listened but knew better than to get involved. He understood my lashing out unreasonably through the burden of pain. The man is so smart he knows better than to contest an unreasonable state of mind. "You need to talk to your husband and tell him how you feel. Just tell him that you don't want to go back and that it's not for you."

"It's not that simple. He's bullheaded and doesn't hear me."

"You're an adult. You don't have to do anything you don't want to."

That afternoon I did talk to my husband and no, he didn't really hear me. The reply was made, "We don't have to go back if you don't want to, but I think we should at least give it another try. Let's wait and see if Adam and Eve send an email first. Have you checked the computer lately? Maybe they've sent something now." My husband was on the prowl and wanted more.

Monday morning I checked the computer as usual and sure enough they had sent an email. Eve sent a very nice compacted note. 'Had a good time, looking forward to two weeks.' It was short sweet and to the point with little emotion. Afternoon rolled around and another email arrived. This time it was from Adam. 'Enjoyed Saturday night. I think about it throughout the day and it brings a smile to my face. Looking forward to our next meeting.' Well, it went something like that. The note was a little longer. Like my husband Adam had enjoyed the sexual encounter immensely. Well crap. What was I to do now?

Two Saturday's later we did go back and yes Adam and Eve were there waiting for us so we sat with the couple from the beginning of the evening. During the drive my husband and I had had a long talk and discussed the matter that I did not want that man's hands all over me again. I then begged him to not stay until closing time.

"That's fine," he replied, "We don't have to stay to the end if you don't want to. Just nudge me and let me know." Sure, but pray tell when has that tactic ever worked?

Conversation started out respectively with Adam and Eve. Many things were said like 'we don't go to the back room every time we're here'. That was a load off the mind while taking some of the sexual pressure off.

Watching the sexy dancers on the floor I suddenly made an upbeat comment. "One of my fantasies is to dance provocatively and tease the guys." Stupid me, that's what all the girls do here, the mere nature of this place. But I didn't have enough gumption and self esteem to pull off the fantasy. Eve went out to dance by herself and began talking with other girls while pulling off my fantasy with ease. It's most likely at this point that I began to cower within my shell. I hated this place and didn't want to be here and yes, Adam's hands were all over me. They caressed up my thighs and under my mini skirt and over my hips. But at times he also did this to the girl sitting next to us. She just grinned and put up with it too.

I made every excuse in the book to get up and move around, first to the restroom, the soda bar, the snack table, and talk to the DJ. Too bad the chocolate covered strawberries were gone this time. I drank too much amaretto that night, not enough to get drunk but just enough to promote a headache.

Late in the evening my husband and I sat together while talking. Searching for his thoughts I spoke first. "Doesn't look like Eve is interested tonight."

"No, I don't think so either."

"I think she's got a case of attitude going on."

"I don't know about that," he replied like a typical man.

Something was going on. Guess my uninterested signals were coming through loud and clear and she was there to have fun whether I was or not. I was ready to leave.

"It's about midnight," I said giving the strong hint.

"Oh, let's stay a little longer. Things might get interesting."

That angle always makes me mad. What in this vast creation could get interesting at this point? Possibly the nude dance contest in the dance cage was interesting or the young couple on the floor. The young wife was drunk as a skunk behaving as though she were in dire need of carnal relief. Another young woman tried to help her out, but was not getting the job done. Suddenly the young husband grabbed his wife situating her in a position on the floor while burying his head between her legs to provide assistance. That is until the owner of the club came past quickly stating, "Not here, you have to take that to the back rooms."

Adam's hands continued to roam over my back and shoulders until Eve came along. I tried not to stare as she suddenly straddled him. I couldn't see but everyone knew his hand had found its way inside her panties and he was fingering her as she silently writhed and squirmed. Earlier as she danced he had smiled at me and said, "Isn't she great?" I could tell that was his expression again as he gave her satisfaction.

At this point I begged my husband to leave until it perturbed him. He had held off for about an hour and a half and then we finally got ready to depart. Eve more or less brushed us off in the departure and when her husband closed in to kiss me on the lips I escaped. No more emails from them. Good.

On the way home I told my husband never again, I would never step foot in that place ever again. But regrettably I must admit we did go two more times in the fall, only after he blackmailed me with offer of a sports car.

# Chapter 7

Isn't it wonderful when a spouse goes on vacation leaving you home all alone to enjoy peace and quiet for yourself? Fourth of July weekend my spouse was going to be gone from Friday morning until Monday noon, quite a long weekend leaving the mouse with plenty of time to play.

"No sweetheart I can't make it to New York when he's gone," Ray listened to my explanation, "I have to stay here and take care of the livestock but you would be more than welcome to come visit here." The innovated response just slipped out of my mouth.

"Yeah, I could fly out there again."

What an exciting thought, Ray visiting this home where I could treat him like the royal king that he is, just the two of us all alone in the house while leaving me with the ability to carry on with daily responsibilities. Spending time here he could see all the things that I rattled on about day after day, as well as visit the historic town that I was born in. Oh, and meet my family and everything! Quite a naïve image? Believe me there were many doubts about pulling off this fantastic feat.

Of course with exuberant challenge in mind the obvious question was pondered of how to accomplish this wild adventure. It could be done. Surely there was a way. I would have to drive to the airport after my husband left for the ball park Friday morning. Ray would just have to wait at the airport until I could safely get away. And then the kicker would be how to get Ray back to the airport before my husband came home. I would have to cover something else up with a farfetched tale. There was also a small issue concerning the neighbors. Would they see a strange man at my house and in the yard? Ray would have to smoke outside and still yet cigarette smell might linger inside so we would also have to hide the cigarette butts after he left.

"Honey," Ray said distracting my ramblings, "why can't you just tell the truth?"

"Huh?"

"Why can't you just tell him the truth?"

"The truth?"

"He knows that we're friends. What's wrong with just saying that I'll be there for a visit?"

"Oh." The rambling thought processes suddenly came to a grinding halt. Wow, telling the truth for a change. What an unbelievably striking concept he had there! "I suppose that would work." Me, telling the truth for a change? Besides, lies were getting old and more difficult with time. I was undoubtedly ready for change in this venue, so now talks of the bi-curious girl that I had spent weekends with suddenly ended as they fell off the edge of the cliff and disappeared forever. This was going to be a new existence, no more lies, maybe.

I don't remember at what point my husband realized that I had a friend named Ray who called on the phone occasionally. They also spoke to one another, occasionally even became consumed in long conversations on the phone. Both men can be big talkers. They discuss ballgames, weather and tease me while holding the majority rule. So what if I have tons of energy and bounce off the walls some days?

Bringing up this topic of Ray's visit to my husband needed careful timing. Delicate matters such as this usually require waiting until he deliriously refers to young strippers with a smile plastered across his tanned face. Sunday morning's are best to bring up intricate situations concerning my boyfriends. It was after hubby went on and on about some young girl's flirtation I suddenly mentioned the idea of Ray visiting our home. He didn't say much. There was perhaps a grunt finished with silence so I said nothing more. It was best to let the idea settle for awhile. Later there was reinforcement of the idea with a positive image. "It would be fun to show Ray the Midwest."

By the third reinforcement my husband finally acknowledged the idea with more than a manly grunt so I pushed the issue, "You will have the car so I'll drive the truck to the airport and pick him up. Then Monday evening we can all go to the fireworks together." He finally accepted this scenario. We had plans for Ray to visit our home. I would be alone with my boyfriend for two and a half days and three nights. My husband would be home on Monday but he would have to go to work Tuesday morning, so Ray and I would have another moment to be alone before we returned to the airport on Tuesday.

The dynamics of this completely bazaar episode is unbelievable. This one took the cake. How many people involved in an affair can go out on a limb and bring their lover into their home, and with the spouses blessing? This was simply too far out. But it's only the beginning. No, my husband did not know that Ray was my boyfriend and therefore suspected nothing out of the ordinary, or sexually. And during Ray's visit my husband did not have a clue. It was only after the fact that a bit of information was stunningly revealed.

I drove that long two hour and fifteen minute drive to the airport concerned that five hours on the road was going to kill me by that evening but it didn't. Ray helped drive back home and we had a blast. He put a CD in the player and we just talked and talked all the way home. Once we got to my house things were a little different than when we arrived at the little cabin. We didn't fall into each other's arms at that very moment.

Ray and I walked through the house as I showed him where everything was. He dropped his luggage off in the computer room near the daybed where he would sleep. We then made a tour of the farm as he learned the names of all the livestock. The friendly ones made up to him quite quickly. He's a magnate for pets and babies so he says and it is true. I'm sure the neighbors noticed us walking around but since we rarely talk I don't know if they thought much at all.

Aspects of our very close relationship changed a little while in my home or shall we say in my husband's home. Ray was in another man's castle embracing the king's wife. Perhaps it is understandable that we took things a little slower. But yes, it was still daylight when we fell into the daybed together and it felt good. Strangely enough at night it just worked out that we did not sleep together. He took my bed while I took the master bedroom. It was nice to have my bed back again without the chainsaw snore. Possibly we followed through with these sleeping arrangements just in case my husband should suddenly show up in the middle of the night. It was the proper thing to do.

How many people would be foolish enough or even have enough gumption to do what we did? This situation is completely unreal to most I can only imagine. Never would they allow a lover over for the weekend. How could two people be so careless . . . no, so gutsy to pull this stunt off? Different circumstances I suppose. Remember my newly found image was to now tell most everyone the truth. Ray and I were friends, sure with benefits but friends just the same. There is one more startling revelation yet to come. My husband did find something out.

Saturday evening we had dinner plans with my sister. Quite excited we drove to her town as dusk descended over the land. There we met her and my feisty godchild at the local Mexican restaurant. Conversation flowed smoothly as I was with my favorite people and dialogue flowed easily between the other three as they are great talkers. No one seemed to be uncomfortable in the exchange as I sat there with my boyfriend instead of husband. We enjoyed ourselves immensely and the food was great as usual.

At the end of the meal sis unexpectedly stated, "We were going to rent a movie this evening. Would you like to come over and watch it with us?"

I didn't have a chance to reply as Ray jumped on the statement. "Sure, that'd be great." It was me that felt suddenly strange but there was no harm in just going to sis's house to watch a movie.

In the countryside, referred to by many locals as God's country, Ray marveled at the big farm, its buildings and the old farmhouse. Not something that he viewed on a regular basis in New York and the Midwest truly opened his eyes. That's what makes vacations interesting, seeing different sights and taking in the flavor of new cultures.

It was just the three of us that watched the movie in the living room. My godchild left to go upstairs to chat with friends in instant messenger, and my brother-in-law did not get home from his meeting until we were gone late in the evening. So while watching the suspense thriller Ray and I snuggled on the couch as sis took the recliner closer to the television. It was mildly strange to be in her presence with a different man and she later remarked that she felt the same. But it was as though she had known him for a while since our talks had been in such great depth, besides the fact that she had also previously spoke to Ray on the phone a couple of times.

The movie ended with a fantastic twist to the plot and we three sat there startled but joking just the same. How crazy and creative some writers can be, how wonderful is that?

Our evening ended with vocalized expectations of Monday's Fourth of July celebration, a positive exchange.

Sunday morning Ray and I stirred about slowly, played on the computer, made love again and then prepared to go out for the day. By noon we were definitely ready to get out of the house. Plans had been made earlier to tour the local countryside, the farmland six miles out. We took a quick drive around the Amish area all the while he threatened to walk up to an Amish man, smile and say, "Hey! Wuz up? What's happening? I'm from New York! Nice to meet ya!"

"Please, don't embarrass me," I begged my bold and brazen boyfriend. "The Amish are quiet people. They know everyone. They might even know me." It is true. They could have very well known my vehicle and identified it with my in-laws. The principal being that since they don't have television for distraction communication runs rampant through the community and it does.

We drove past a large Amish farm, white clapboard house, clean and pristine, farm animals all about. A gathering of local people congregated for church that morning in this particular home, their black buggies parked at the gravel entrance to the barn. It was the perfect setting of Amish life for Ray to see. There was even a gentleman with suspenders, crisp white shirt and black hat adjusting the harness of the buggy horse. Thank goodness my boyfriend only observed and did not yell greetings from the window.

By early afternoon we were in my historic hometown. We toured the large limestone memorial situated over the sight of the old fort, and walked around the first brick house built in this area of the Louisiana territory, home to one of our first few presidents. The day was a sizzling hot one and Ray eventually suggested something from Dairy Queen. It was a welcome relief to sit down together and relax with something cold.

I have to say quickly that we know of another gentleman, Mr. Butterworth that chats in our favorite room. The next day, while online, we teased Mr. Butterworth that we saw him from the Dairy Queen window. He laughed while hoping that Ray was enjoying his vacation here in the Midwest. Small world that we live in.

That evening I fixed a spaghetti dinner and afterwards we relaxed on the living room floor with a rented movie, and then made love before going to bed.

Monday noon came and I think Ray was a bit nervous. If he was apprehensive he didn't show it but I do believe a small amount of tension was there. My husband would be home any time now. Ray and I had quickly enjoyed one another earlier that morning and then showered preparing for my husband's homecoming. We were in the kitchen a little after noon when car doors could suddenly be heard. I swiftly looked at Ray with sheer terror in my eyes. We had forgotten something. A tell tale sign from our early morning tryst lay on the floor beside the daybed. Ray and I both ran to the room and shoved the item under the bed and then ran back to kitchen where we resumed a casual atmosphere. Maybe it was a bad sign to scare Ray in that manner, completely unintentional. I do feel bad but he handled matters just fine. And then maybe again the rush of adrenalin was invigorating and exciting, quite daring to boot. I believe he enjoys the thrill of challenge as much as I do. He has to enjoy it especially dating a married woman while sitting in the home of her husband.

The climactic moment was abruptly upon us. The world stood still for a minute as the two men met, shook hands and introduced themselves. I slowly faded into the background unable to get a word in edgewise. Equally vocal in formalities of conversation they volleyed back and forth. This went on a little longer than my husband was accustomed to as I watched him tire, but it was unnoticed to our guest. Within the hour my husband was able to take a few moments to unpack the suitcase and recover from the long drive. That afternoon he returned to the kitchen/living room area and I suddenly fell into the background again while the two men retired to watch a ballgame on television. This transaction went so smoothly. It was utterly remarkable as I smiled while shaking my head.

I now had some free time to myself for a bit and started a load of laundry and then straightened up the house. At one point during their ballgame on the television I offered them ice cream sandwiches. Oh this was just way too ironic, my two men getting along famously although my husband didn't have a clue . . . yet.

By evening the tone began to change as extra company in our home was wearing thin on my husband's nerves. He managed to put on a brave front but felt that his privacy was a little infringed upon. Ray didn't notice a thing but I saw the changes and felt the difficulties. My husband's discomfort was wearing on me a little too.

Grilling out that evening before heading out to Fourth of July festivities we sat at the patio table as conversations continued to flow freely. That is until my husband suddenly stated that the rose bush is too large. Ray, becoming uncomfortably, saw the marital antagonism growing toward one another. Perhaps it's my attention deficit disorder which makes me unable to sit still for very long, or maybe it's that my husband thinks I should jump when he makes a comment. But anyway I jumped up and began pruning back the rose bush in a complete huff. Ray was uncomfortable. My husband barked out 'you don't have to do that now'. It's sad that our guest had to suddenly experience our disengaged way of living, or antagonism. Our guest wasn't the first to see the discord. Friends and family have seen it too.

Dinner went fine and dishes were quickly put away as I was in a hurry to meet up with family that evening. But hubby dragged his feet. He had to take a shower first and then slowly got ready. I pushed every chance I could find and helped him retrieve clothes from the closet while hastily putting on makeup too. Ray was unfortunately in the middle of the confusion while just talking away. My husband suddenly pulled me aside and asked, "What he is doing in our bedroom while we're trying to get ready?"

"It's just this one time thing. Maybe it's because he's been using this shower."

"And why has he been using this shower? What about the guest room shower?"

"I don't know. That's your bathroom. Maybe he didn't want to infringe upon your space."

"It's a guest shower that's what it's for. I don't like the idea of him using this bathroom."

"Don't worry about it. Ray will just be here one more night. Hurry up because my family is going to be waiting for us. We're going to be late as it is."

The drive didn't go much better. Both men were in the front seat which left me in the back. Ray remarks to this day that backseat driving never looked so ugly. "Can't you drive faster?" I asked completely rushed. The cell phone suddenly rang, it was sis. "Yes, we'll be there as quick as we can. I'm sorry that you have to wait! Someone had to take a shower first. Just wait for us and we'll be there in 20 minutes . . . I know it looks like rain. I'm sorry that you guys wanted to see the fireworks over the Ohio River . . . . You had free tickets? Ok fine, it's all my fault." And then once we were ready to leave the freeway I barked out, "No, don't take this exit go to the next one."

Thank goodness Ray met my family a lot more smoothly than the drive went. Even my brother-in-law that wasn't fond of my inappropriate marital antics welcomed my boyfriend with great fanfare. Dad, mom, sis and the kids all made him feel welcome into the little family pod. Ray and I walked side by side along the long sidewalk to our family's favorite spot for watching fireworks, but then hubby set his chair on the other side of me wishing to be close and probably feeling a strange dynamic in the air. At one point hubby even took my hand to hold it in his. I was flustered. Ray laughed at the simple gesture thinking it was cute however I felt like marked property, quite uncomfortable to say the least.

The evening quickly ended on a positive note when dad invited Ray to return next year for the popular Memorial Day festival, but the most striking thing that was said that night came from mom as she remarked, "He's got the nicest blue eyes."

Ray continues mentioning to this day with a smile, "Mom likes me." Mom does respect Ray and inquires about his well being from time to time.

Tuesday evening, vacation was over, and Ray was on a plane almost back to the state of New York when hubby came home from work. I don't remember how the conversation got started but he asked, "Did anything happen while I was gone?" We were now on the conversation of sex. I just smiled from the kitchen as he stood in the hall.

Hubby continued, "So I take it that something happened."

Remember my new tactics were to not lie for a change. My heart pounded but I had rehearsed this very confrontation. "Yup."

"Once?"

"Once on the living room floor while we watched the movie."

"So there was a second time?"

"Yes, just twice," I lied. I didn't want to destroy him right then and there although he took the information quite well. There were no details, only reference to the fact that yes there had been sex in the house with Ray's visit.

"Did you plan this all along?" My husband asked out of concern.

Yes, we knew it would happen but I told him, "No, it was not planned, but you know I wanted to be with another man while I still have the chance, before I'm too old. It just happened. Besides, you told me that I could be with another man at the swingers club if the opportunity presented itself." That was true. He had no reason to reprimand me on that point. He has the physical presence of strippers every Saturday night draped across his shoulder. "And remember, it was a year ago when you said I could have sex with Steve or Brad if the opportunity presented itself."

He didn't seem to hear that last part as he continued, "But I thought we agreed if anything happened we would do it together."

"Yes, I know, but this situation is a little different. I know him. It's not like we're strangers or something. I think it's actually better to know someone if you're going to be with them."

My husband didn't scold me for my actions nor did he think any less of Ray, an outcome that I am exceptionally grateful for. Wouldn't you think that a large percentage of husband's would belittle the man that had sex with their wife while alone in their home? He didn't have a fit, thankfully.

Surprisingly there is one more thing, one more revelation that most men would seem to have a problem with, in fact, most would probably have an out and out battle over this matter. During a weeknight evening we were discussing sex. A simple thought crossed my mind and then I giggled. He asked what it was. I hesitated at first, but he asked for it.

I purred, "Mmm, Italian men. Ray is part Italian."

He had to think a little. He is all German, but then suddenly realized the implication of Italian men. "Where does that leave me?"

"No," I tried to correct, "You are just fine. It's like strippers come in different shapes and sizes. Men are built differently too. Let's just say that some Italian men have a little thickness."

"Now I really feel inferior."

I hugged him while trying to sooth his feelings. "We're doing just fine. There's nothing wrong with our sex." Of course my thoughts are mixed on the matter but perhaps some things, negative repercussions of porn addiction should just remain quiet. Both men are different. As humans we all have preferences and ideals. There is no right and wrong as long as satisfaction and culmination have their place and time.

Was that last line diplomatic or what? I do enjoy the feeling of my husband's strong shoulders and large protective arms around me and I told him so, so there.

But on the other hand, does he realize what my words could do? Why doesn't he fight back? Words paired together in certain prose are capable of destroying a person, ruining a valuable life. I could never destroy anyone.

I am able to accomplish this feat but would never go to that extreme. The karma of negativity would dog me for eternity creating pure hell.

I feel capable of destroying and damaging a person though, just ask Steve. Never before have I thrown such illegal punches repeatedly toward another. Thankfully his hide is very thick. I was only mad because he would not stop asking for nude pictures. He actually blackmailed to the point of saying 'give me a picture or I'm leaving'. It was either give him what he wanted or he refused to chat. That is totally rude of the man and he should stand accused for the crime.

Concerning my husband this attempt at truthfulness continued by the time I wanted to go back to New York. He did allow a long weekend in New York that November and again in March of the next year. After that March Ray and I would not see each other for over a year. It pulled on the heart strings of our relationship a few times during that year. It certainly was a difficult span of many months.

Oh, and I did get a sweatshirt that has New York plastered across the front of it. We purchased it in November on the day he introduced me to Woodbury Commons, a designer outlet mall north of the city. My favorite store there? Waterford Crystal of course. In March of the next year I purchased Stuart crystal instead. The vase that was chosen is prettier than the comparable Waterford if that's any excuse.

But to summarize all of this you must realize that my husband has allowed Ray to be part of my life, part of our lives. I have been allowed to have sex with another man and visit that man's house as well, even after revelation of the sexual fact from that Fourth of July. Why would a caring husband allow such things to happen? Is it his guilt and inability to say anything in the matter? If his secret journey's to strip clubs were to be found out by friends and family it would be his guilt and disgrace on the line, all this garbage for the sake of sexuality. What a shame that a formable life needs to hide behind such a façade, especially when the addiction lessens the ability to truly live a fulfilling married life, mentally as well as physically.

Perhaps the reader might allow my eccentricities to step forward for a moment as I try to explain another view on—shall we say straying from a marriage? Bear with me as the topic touches off on religion for starters.

All forms of worship begin with Christian, Jewish, Mennonite, Amish, Catholicism, Methodist, Baptist, Buddhism, the Great White Spirit . . . to simply name a few. It's all good if the result is a heart full of hope and respect for one another. However it's a shame when some religions clash together in the form of military battle over inability to get along, but the subsequent malady is not where we are going.

Each religion acknowledges to its people that their traditions and values are the best and should be held and professed to all, or witnessed toward others as some might say. Does that seem dangerous to anyone else, religion bad mouthing another religion? Where is the status of God in the center of this debate on traditions?

And so the people listen to their elders and attend church every Sunday morning along with Saturday night mass, Wednesday night worship, and Friday night Bible study. (I will not reveal the one ladies group that got caught by the minister as they hid the bottle of wine in the church basement. Shame on you, you fun filled feisty ladies. God be with you as you go forth into the world. Perhaps you should try the white wine next time, white being pure and angelic.)

So, if we proclaim that one religion is the best and tend to ignore the rest what are we actually saying about our existence as a whole? Isn't this world one? No. It is divided and divided and one more divided into infinite divisions. Sorry, I tend to gush.

This world, this planet earth is split into so many sectors of so many different kinds of people professing so many different things . . . Have you ever looked at the stars in the night sky and felt like such a small being, a little ant in the mass of thousands of years in the history of mankind. Your thoughts, your opinions on any trivial matter in this universe are just that, your own. And if you are not a president, a pope or a king your voice is heard by few.

Now that we have narrowed ourselves back to this one square foot of ground that we stand upon. What matters? What actually matters to the masses? Survival . . . living . . . living the best that we can, it is the only thing of concern.

I must also state that I'm an advocate for the health of this planet. There is only one ancient religion that I see. The basic principal of thought is to take only what you need from the earth and give back so that the next generation can survive as well. What's so wrong with that, give and take? It is therefore simply stated yet so difficult to see.

How does this pattern of contemplation coincide with my attempt at allowing one to stray from the sanctity of marriage? If the multitude of religions cannot view another's tradition as being acceptable then where do we draw the line at accusation? Are churches accusing other churches of not teaching propriety correctly enough? On a whole they are doing the proper thing, teaching the word of God, gathering together, witnessing together, but I think this is missing the mark. God created the earth. Let's protect it together as one religion, as a whole. If we all came from Adam and Eve (which I also believe is a parable) then lets get back to being a whole and protect one another, give and take. Yeah, I know, this fantasy will never happen.

Although I have broken one of the Ten Commandments . . . what am I saying? Heck, I've broken more than one. I still believe that my relationship with Ray is blessed from a higher realm. It has to be since we provide such deep emotional support for each other.

Oh brother, am I going to get opposition on this or what? Therefore it must quickly be added that an opinion should be valued whether agreed upon or not. I value an opinion too, believe me, it is the best way to learn with learning being a valuable tool and all.

My husband and I went to the swinger club two more times. (Yes, we're off the topic of religion now with a heading in the opposite direction.) He had to blackmail me with 'I'll buy you the sports car that you want only if you go to the swinger club'. It was time to trade off the ten year old car anyway, but he was serious nonetheless. I gave in to the venture with stipulation that if Adam and Eve were at the club we would ignore them. There was certainly no love lost there for either party. Also, if allowances were going to be made for another trip to New York in November I needed to let my husband receive his jollies once again. So this journey to the swinger club was simply a bartered trade off for both of us.

Wearing comfortable jeans and dressy tee shirt that night I swore no bloody idiot was going to get his hands all over me this time. The protective chain mail was firmly in place surrounding my shoulders like a well worn sweater, and no, Adam and Eve were not there that evening. What a great break. First things first as a creature of habit I hit the chocolate covered strawberries, relishing the tasty treat.

Atmosphere was different this night, bearable in its own way. Faces were also different except for three or four couples we had seen before. One of the gals that had devoured another girl that first night was in here. Her date was the same guy too. Something wasn't right though, they just didn't look right together. He was older, never smiled and reminded me of the mere essence of Dracula. She has a great body, long straight hair and glasses, is most likely a sweetheart but not my husband's type so he never encouraged her attention.

A new person, female, sat next to my husband this evening. Her date seemed very nervous and again they didn't seem like an actual couple. This big gal was not my husband's type either, not cute bubbly or curvaceous, but they conversed off and on throughout the evening. I was just glad hubby had someone else to talk to.

This certain large woman was a close friend to the owners, most likely a stripper in her day when the building was used as a strip club, and she eventually spoke of having a daughter that danced at one of the local strip clubs.

That mere fact caught my husband's attention as they conversed over matters I could not hear. I wasn't interested anyway since this excursion was to just pay my dues for more demanding issues like the car and another trip out east.

Time progressed into the evening and we danced a little, watched people for awhile before he asked, "Want to go to the back rooms?" Actually this was after a young couple sitting on my side of the table had stated that they were going to the back rooms 'just to watch'.

"Why?"

"Just to look around."

"No, I really don't want to go."

"Come on, let's go. Maybe we can go into a room ourselves."

"Hmm," I thought. "Maybe, but I wouldn't want anyone to watch us."

"No one will watch us."

"You can't be so sure. You don't know."

He begged, "Come on, let's just go."

And so we slipped into the cavern of delights. There were a few other couples engulfed in the dark domain. Some of the small lamps were turned off and I supposed there were lovers inside. Two or three other rooms contained couples that left the lamps on and one could glance inside while viewing their eroticism and hearing it too. Farther back there was an empty room which my husband and I slipped past the beads and sheer black veil. We got comfortable on the couch as roaming hands began to arouse, and then clothes started coming off.

"Here put this sheet down on the couch." I stated.

"What for?" He asked.

"Because that's what they're here for. It's what you're supposed to do."

"Oh."

"And I'm turning off the lamp."

"But you're not supposed too."

"I don't want anyone looking in," I sternly held my ground while flipping the switch. It is a good thing that I did turn off the little lamp because as soon as we became engulfed in one another someone did come to stand at our doorway while gawking. I swear to this day that it was the Dracula looking guy and his girl. I'm so afraid that as a swinger he would have liked to join us. Shivering from horror at the mere thought.

But you know it wasn't so bad after all, sex in semi-public with my husband. Actually I didn't know he could move like that while having sex on a couch, and was seriously astounded that he could still change positions quickly. Mmm, I liked that, something different and new. Afterward it was sort of strange going back into the lounge, but by then girls had gone wild on the dance floor so there was no need for shyness.

Toward the end of the evening the owner announced over the loud speaker for all couples to take a chair to the center of the dance floor. What was about to happen? This was off the wall and something totally new. Would it embarrass me?

We took one chair to the center of the floor and placed it in a line with several other couples, all faces were curious of the owner's intentions.

He teased, "I bet you are all wondering what we're going to do? Line your chairs up first. Alright, men sit down. Ladies," the announcer paused, "stand in front of your men. You're going to give him a lap dance."

Oh fun! The music came on and I gave it my best shot. Sure I'm no longer 20 years old or a professional strip artist but gave it my best shot while wiggling and stretching about. Hubby smiled although I wasn't quite sure if it actually turned him on or not. Nonetheless we had fun and most of all we were doing this together. No one else was involved.

When the song was over the announcer called out, "Alright, men stand up. Ladies sit down. Men, you are going to give her your best lap dance." What a roar of laughter ensued with that tall order. Well, hubby gave it his best shot.

Sweetheart, just don't quit your day job thinking dirty dancing is a lucrative business. I was completely charmed that he gave it his all. Oh, and I don't play fair during dances because touching is way too much fun. *Wink*

As the evening ended the owners walked through the isles with tickets held high in the air. "Last chance to get your tickets for the Halloween masquerade ball!"

Hubby begged, pleaded, and swore allegiance to whatever, "Please, let's go to the Halloween party. It will be fun." A couple of women he had spoken with earlier reinforced that this particular party would be an excellent one to attend. They had fun with it every year.

I begged, pleaded and swore to his basic nature of human kindness that if you love me, "Please, don't make me go."

He purchased the tickets and we went to the Halloween party.

My nerves were on end. This was one of their really popular parties with a huge attendance. If Adam and Eve were there I would just freakin croak and fall off to the wayside. Thank goodness they were not there or even the other couple that we failed to find common ground with.

At the glass front door I asked of the man with the sign-in clip board. "Is everyone dressed up in costumes?"

He feigned a smile. "Yes they are."

"Oh no," I cried since I was wearing jeans again. But he was only teasing. I didn't realize at the time and halfway down the hall toward the red doors I let a swear word slip out from under my breath. From behind us the man chuckled out loud over my discomfort. I was all ready to become irritated and bent out of sorts knowing that this evening was going to suck, but inside the building it proved that I was not the only one without a costume. Whew.

Do you remember mention of the Dracula looking guy? Yup, he was dressed like Dracula and his girl wore a mini skirt with push up bra, same long straight hair to her waist and those glasses. There was another cute couple dressed up as a French maid and Mr. Clean which they also won for best costume that evening. I couldn't help but stare at him due to his short height and shaved head. That bad boy look reminded me of Ray whom I wished was there with me. Little did I know at the time my husband was watching the curvy frame of the little French maid. She was very cute, petite, young, blonde and his type.

People watching was definitely the name of the game this evening and being at a sex club . . . well; you can only expect a wild crowd. There was an oriental lady on the arm of a big burly good ole boy. He did not seem interested in being there, was very quiet and reserved. She seemed like a lovely lady having a good time but her well formed breasts kept falling out of her extremely tight little black dress but she didn't care. Then there were the newbie's that came in on the tour—a super attractive couple, young, both very tall and overly dressed in brightly colored overalls. In another corner was another bald man, not bad looking. He smoked like a chimney, nervous as a cat on a hot tin roof while his attractive wife was dressed only in a sheer red robe. She proceeded to get very drunk or was maybe was even high on some added element. Either way she was out of it, quite oblivious to one on one communication from anyone including her husband. Perhaps this is why he looked as nervous as a cat.

The dance floor was continually packed this evening with sexy ladies strutting their stuff, plus the one slender gal dressed as Cat Lady. This middle aged woman had all the right moves as she swayed and pawed over other girls. Her tall distinguished and seemingly wealthy husband had my attention. I know what I like. Furthermore he was wearing an expensive suit with tie. The new Corvette sitting outside in the parking lot had to belong to this couple.

The owner of the club suddenly made an announcement over the intercom while small pieces of paper were quickly noticed sitting next to the Halloween candy on everyone's table. "Alright everyone, we have an exciting game to play tonight." Actually this was an activity to get us stick in the muds out of our seats and walking around introducing themselves to one another. I felt bold and brazen and ready for the stimulating challenge.

The man continued. "Each piece of paper has four symbols on it. Your job is to find the person holding the exact match to all four of yours."

Instantly people were randomly conversing with the next guy. My husband wasn't interested in playing so I got up from the seat and began wandering around the room asking different players if we matched. Oh, and we signed our names to the back of the other person's paper while becoming familiar with each other. I talked to several persons that evening. There was the couple that we had seen during our second trip to the club. This woman had sat on the other side of Adam as he caressed up her thighs and under her miniskirt. I spoke to her husband for a few moments. He seemed like a nice Midwestern gentleman polite and mostly quiet. And then there was a little guy in a cowboy hat that I had possibly glanced at too long. He had the brightest big blue eyes. I think he was extremely interested as I felt his eye sight following me after our exchange, but I was not attracted or interested. Slowly but surely I made my way across to the other side of the dance floor—to where the man in the expensive business suit sat.

Seeing that he was alone I asked while wishing to compare symbols, "Are you playing the game?" Sadly he failed to look me in the eye.

"No, but I think they are at the next table." Brush off was quickly complete.

I slowly made my way back around the crowd and got a couple more names. It had been an interesting diversion, something that thankfully got me out of my seat.

Conga line! Who would ever pass up a conga line? So much fun. We joined in the long dance line somewhere along the middle of crowded mass hysteria. My husband held onto my shirt and he clearly remembers the oriental gal behind him struggling to keep up. Too bad he couldn't see whether her dress remained in place or not. My guess is that it did not stay in place and therefore she most likely bounced all about.

It seems like the crazy antics went on for several minutes, a good way to pass some more time. Then the conga line slowly died out to only a few people left on the dance floor. We sat down and then suddenly my eyes bugged out as the woman in the sheer red robe laid sprawled out on the floor. In position on her back with legs open the remaining conga line took turns imitating sex over her, male and female. In a corner her nervous husband continued to chain smoke one after another until he finally went out to the floor to pull her away. She was none to happy about his interference and weakly fought against his restraining hand. Her condition had to be induced by more than only alcohol, it was just too strange.

Midnight or after, the place normally closes around 2 am, although tonight would most likely be open a little later. Hubby asked to go to the back rooms but without the implication of sex this round. We stepped into the first room and were quickly approached by another couple. I had not noticed them this earlier evening. They were from far from home and were staying at a local hotel so it was stated. The man was a good ole boy type in a plaid shirt and jeans, not polished around the edges and not my type in the least. His wife was very pretty at first glance, peaches and cream complexion, beautiful pale blonde hair, petite and about my same height . . . and she was very interested in me. They were into foursome, threesome, girl on girl or whatever we liked.

The men stood side by side in the isle conversing quite well while she and I sat on the coffee table. I tried not to stare into the room in front of me where sex was going on albeit with the dim light off.

Her husband stood in front of us while stating his cause, "I never push anyone into anything they don't want to do. I always wait and let a lady lead me with whatever she likes. Respecting others is important to us but we do have a hotel room if you guys are interested."

And the wife began her case, "My dad is a minister but they don't know how we are. Do you have any piercings?"

"Oh no." I quickly replied. "Just pierced ears." It was now noticed that her tongue was pierced. Oh, I bet she likes girls.

"Both my nipples are pierced too. Would you like to see?"

"No, that's ok." Oh my gosh! I cringed with the idea of pain.

My husband didn't help matters and lead them on while vividly imagining the next step of his porn addiction, thinking maybe we had a future with this couple. We got up to walk along the hallway to peek into the rooms. It was rather noisy tonight and as we approached the white room it was now noticed why the noise factor was high. It was the sex swing. The two newbie's that had been wearing brightly colored overalls were going at it full consummation. Totally naked he was pounding as she moaned loudly with every forceful thrust, bouncing off him, totally relishing one another. It was hot and one would have to be a eunuch to not be affected by the sight and sound. There was another couple on the couch with the man thrusting from on top.

We didn't stand there long since it's not polite so we stepped aside. The four of us stopped in the hallway in front of the restrooms for a moment. I was finished with the evening now and ready to get out of this joint but the girl continued to work on my attention along with her husband. She showed me her nipple piercings, quite proud of them but it seems like such a needless pain to endure. Perhaps we exchanged email addresses at this point. Memory has slipped on the facts although I do remember I dumped their address in the nearest wastebasket. She did not email me either.

On the way out of the back rooms I peeked into the white room once more. The tall girl was still in the swing, legs wrapped around her man. He leaned into her, hugging her as they tried catching their breath, in each other's arms right where they should be, loving one another and not in the arms of a stranger.

Gathering my purse and bottle of amaretto from our table I noticed my husband staring at the Mr. Clean guy. His country boy stare is weird, quite embarrassing and was most likely turning Mr. Clean off.

"Let's go talk to that couple," he stated. "Want to go sit with them for a little while?"

"No. I'm ready to go."

"It won't hurt you for just a few minutes."

"I don't want to."

He suddenly, sharply lashed out accusing, "I hate when you get like this, so damn inflexible."

"Well, you're staring at him an' freaking him out and he probably thinks you're gay."

"He does not. That's ridiculous."

"They're probably listening to us argue too. It's no use. Let's go home."

"Why can't you ever do things my way?"

"I've just spent an hour giving some chick the wrong impression that I might be interested when I'm not. I'm not about to start giving another person the wrong idea that there's hope when there's not. Besides that couple is only into each other. They're not interested in us."

"You don't know that."

Sigh.

I knew it was time to quit playing these games that were getting us no where, not getting my husband any closer to what he wanted. I realize that this life style is not going to happen so I said 'no more'. We were foolishly leading people on by giving hopes that were not my hopes. Besides the fact that my husband was becoming an embarrassment to me with persistence of 'lets talk to this couple or that' especially when his manner of speech is so countrified.

He has now found out that he can have more than one membership to the club. A member can have several memberships with different partners. (Perhaps this is why some couples did not look right together because they are not really married or permanent partners.) Lovely—guess this only supports the word swinger. I don't care. More power to him. Just don't bring deadly STD's into our home. But in the long run it doesn't look like he is having much luck at employing a new partner to further his addiction. So what holds this marriage together? Perhaps financial security is the glue. We are a business venture, familiarity, family security or pretence of it.

# CHAPTER 8

It's mind boggling how the internet has a little bit of absolutely everything. Like everything you ever wanting to know and then some extra fluff that is just plain weird. The basic saying 'it takes all kinds' could not be truer in some cases. A few of those weird things that come along once in a blue moon suddenly make one take notice plus impulsively inquire 'what the heck was that?' or 'you've got to be kidding'.

The beginning of the following account was vocalized to me so I'm going to be very careful in relaying this unfolding plot. It was June when Ray was busy chatting in the large popular room. 'Superman', a hopeless romantic that seems to have a new girlfriend every week or so, was also in the room hitting on all the cute girls as he continually does so proficiently. These two men have known one another for quite some time and communicate in the room while teasing with reckless banter. Ray joined in wild wordplay with the crazy super hero as words scrolled fast and furiously across the screen, their flirtation totally relished by a few girls. I wasn't around at the time and only heard this account within hours of the particular instance.

In the public chat forum Superman had roughly described some business dealings he's been involved in and on this particular day mention was again made about a job. Ray rapidly asked Superman if he had a position opening to which Superman happily whispered in a private window 'yes I do'. Talks quickly escalated in the private venue and then proceeded to their cell phones. The next thing I realize is that Ray is in my instant messenger typing some sort of passionate promise of a future project.

"Superman's real name is Vinnie," Ray was telling me, "he's from Chicago and he is very rich."

"You don't know for sure, he might just be saying that." I replied skeptical of most internet bragging.

"He's on the phone with me right now."

"Oh." I waited awhile for Ray to begin typing again.

"OMG," he typed on the screen, "you wouldn't believe this guy. He knows some really wealthy people and he wants to give me a job. I could be a millionaire!"

"Sweetheart," I returned across the screen, "slow down, you don't know this guy."

"I know. Hang on. He's busy talking to me. Here check out these web sites."

Ray sent the URL of two addresses and I quickly checked them out. They looked legitimate. Damn, if this information was true then these guys were big time. The first web site was of an executive from out west with an impressive list of achievements in the world of entertainment software. There was even a photo of the man beside his collection of exotic sports cars. One could only drool at the excess of finery. The second finely constructed web site was even more impressive. A few men made up a land development company and Vinnie was the president. They had housing developments all over the country mostly near country clubs, golf courses, marinas and you get the idea. I still wasn't convinced. Web sites can easily be constructed for any reason or means.

Ray remained on the cell phone with Vinnie as well as instant messenger and then suddenly typed some more stuff in our whisper. "Look at this."

There was a copy of an email that was cut and pasted into my whisper box. A gentleman from out East had emailed Vinnie a request of how to proceed with an international project in a third world country. I read the words of 'we will need to establish a power plant and the desalination station before going any further with hotels, casinos and the theme park. The government is in complete compliance and ready to proceed. What needs to be filled in here $_____?'

Whoa! It was extremely impressive. Maybe these guys were big time. Maybe they were for real and Vinnie actually wanted to give Ray this big job. Oh my God, Ray could become a rich and wealthy man! How I hoped all this was true. If anyone deserved this fortunate turn of events it was Ray. Of course selfish reasoning of my own passed through my mind. I'm not sure if they surfaced at that very moment or if they came to light a little later on. Heck, who wouldn't want to join that bandwagon?

Ray gave me one more web site to check out. It was the business site from the man from out East. This corporate group made a living out of creating theme parks. A certain board director from the company had helped form some of the more recent additions to a popular destination in Florida. Proof was in the pudding so to speak. Ray was into something with Vinnie and it looked and felt very real. An hour later Ray called me.

"I'm sorry I couldn't call you earlier but Vinnie was giving me all this information. We were in a three way conversation with different people and he kept putting me on hold while talking business with these other guys. Honey, I could be rich someday."

"You really think he's for real?"

"Yeah, his partner from out west has created this particular software which provides protection for people on the internet. They ran a survey earlier this year to see if there's a need for this kind of software and there is a need for it. Vinnie wants me to run the company as the CEO."

"What! The CEO!" I exclaimed.

"Yes, the CEO! The plan is to sell the software to the major internet providers and go from there. It's meant to protect people on the internet and provide a safety net against predators," Ray quickly rambled on in his excitement. "What they do is sell it as an extra tap on to the original internet providers price at say $50 a year . . ."

I quickly became lost in the ramblings of legalities and break down or of how many millions everyone would make from the lucrative venture, but the figures were astronomical. At the most Ray would make $4.5 million a year and as curator Vinnie would dip into hundreds of millions per year. Of course, that is if the product would become popular enough and sell.

Ray continued, "Vinnie is going to get with me in a couple of weeks to go over everything and then by July 15 we'll have a license for the company."

"But why you?" I asked.

"He says it's because he likes my style."

"Well, you certainly do have style. Why do you think I like you?"

Ray laughed. "Honey, you don't just like me you love me, but thank you and you have style too. Seriously though he thinks I can do the job. I told him about the managerial position at Unionet. We also talked about profits and the fact that I increased them over 100% as manger of the store chain back in the '80's. He's impressed with my portfolio."

"Well, yes I agree you are quite capable of running a company. You would be good in the position."

"He's going to give me a sign on bonus of $150,000."

"Oh my God!"

"Yeah, how cool is that? My kids are going to be so spoiled and so are you."

That was dangerous. It put me over the edge dangling by a thread. I was hooked. Ray was going to spoil me? My Ray that was currently being robbed blind by child support, the child support that Vinnie was going to help him get past the burden of. Vinnie was also going to help him get back on his feet from bankruptcy and clear away all the problems of the past. I only hoped that Vinnie was the magician that he claimed to be. My future was now riding high on this wave of excitement. Ray was going to spoil me. Was this finally going to be my escape from the Midwest that I desired so strongly? Tensions were not yet mounting but the future held a hint of something extraordinary yet to come.

A couple of week's later talks with Vinnie were still fast and furious. Vinnie had been very busy and couldn't get together with Ray to go over matters just yet. Ray was deflated a little while expecting that $150,000 to come through very soon but licensing of the product was still another week away. If Ray could just hold on a while longer but to make matters worse the owner of the little cabin on the lake was pushing. The elderly gentleman wished to retire and move into his house by August 1st and time was moving very fast now. Ray needed the money real soon to make his move into an apartment and he let Vinnie know of the dilemma.

Vinnie had it all covered. No problem, don't worry about it. Spoken like a good ole city boy. He would quite conveniently buy a condo in New York City and move Ray into it. Ray could cover all utilities and if Vinnie wanted a vacation home he had access to visit the condo at anytime.

But, not good enough, Ray hates fast paced city life as well as crazy drivers so he begged Vinnie to buy a condo nearer to his kids. Vinnie sternly held his ground. It was his money. Who could argue? The man firmly stated, "New York is the happening city. You gotta have a nice place to entertain clients. Ray, I understand you're uncomfortable with this right now. It's all overwhelming and new to you. You're not used to managing big sums of money so I'm going to teach you how to be wealthy. When you start making the big bucks I'm going to show you where to put your finances to compound them. You're going to have to spend it to make it so you need to look the part too by living in the city."

Ray held his ground about as firmly as an antique cast iron skillet. His feelings were strongly relayed to the other man that he would not live in the city. There was absolutely no way in hell, so in the long run Vinnie stated that he liked Ray's bold nature and subsequently gave in. It's understandable that if a man wants to be near his family it should be granted. Vinnie also agrees very strongly that God, family and kids come first. So the wealthy businessman gave in and agreed that Ray could have a condo near Kingston. "But you'll need office space too. We'll check out some nice business districts when I go out to New York," Vinnie promised.

During these several fast flying weeks of June and July of 2006 Ray, Vinnie and I chatted quite a bit. The big businessman accepted me quite quickly but behind the scenes he asked Ray, "What the heck are you doing with a married woman?"

Does this mean married women are dangerous, fickle, likely to change their mind with the changing of the wind, or once a cheater always a cheater? Ray defended himself with, "Her husband is addicted to porn and goes to strip clubs every weekend. It's not like you think. She doesn't mess around like that."

Vinnie slowly accepted the answer and seemed to understand subtle differences like everyone else eventually does. Ray has had to explain this situation more than once over the years. I love the fact that what Ray and I share is exceptional and true and will last a long time whether we're together or not. We are right where we need to be in this relationship. It fills a need and the void that we each have. We would be lost if the other was suddenly gone from our life.

Early on it's true that I did try to break away from Ray. One day I told him I needed some space and please don't call me for awhile. That lasted about a day and a half before I finally called him and found out the poor man had been left in a daze from our last phone call. He left home that afternoon while driving without any specific destination in mind. Ending up at a large mall he just walked for hours until his legs ached. By evening he woke up from this horrible daydream, and found himself miles from home so he went to a hotel to spend the night.

When we began talking again Ray explained he knew we were not breaking up but this separation was too much for his emotional state to handle. I felt badly for causing this needless fiasco and apologized profusely. My workload had been heavy at the time and I just needed space from the telephone to get some things out of the way. Well, yes in the back of my mind I was trying to gain some space from this long distance relationship also. And to this day I could still use some space. As a writer I need to be completely alone with my thoughts and creativity. It's the only way to stay on course. (And at this very moment in time I've left the internet on purposely so as to concentrate without the interference of the darn phone.)

And so Ray, Vinnie and I chatted from time to time throughout those summer months.

"Pssst, Lisa," Vinnie typed in the open discussion room.

"Yes?" I inquired.

"Don't tell Ray about last night. Damn, it was great. LOL"

"Wtf," Ray quickly responded, "Fuck you Vinnie. LOL"

I didn't respond because this conversation was between the guys. I let Vinnie tease and torment Ray while my boyfriend actually enjoys the attention. We all laughed at the silly antics.

Vinnie pressed even more, "That red teddy is one hot little number."

"Hmm." Ray was left speechless for once so I typed that Lisa goes to sit by Ray and hugs him to sooth his battered feelings. Ray was quickly eased and the men began bouncing onto the next topic. These men are two fiery minds working like liquid lightening, just bam bam bam in each other's face.

"The business will be up and running in no time."

"It better," Ray pushed in return but Vinnie liked this bold perseverance, the sign of a good leader. And then with big dreams in mind Ray stated, "I'm buying the Saleen. You can keep your Lamborghini."

"Yeah, we'll take the cars out and go pick up the girls along the way."

I told my boyfriend, "I'll come running out the door and give you a big kiss on the lips right there in the driveway."

This was all detrimental to my days of chatting for awhile. Oh, sure, I was having a blast with all the attention from fast talking men that knew how to spoil a woman but the other girls began to get jealous. They noticed heavy flirtation with me residing in the center of the bad boy's attention and started to comment. Comments were polite at first until one girl made a snide remark. Of course we all ignored her but I would remember the ill gesture. The three of us were dominating the busy room while making it difficult for others to enjoy themselves too. Later on Vinnie was also reprimanded behind my back by certain girls which he did not stand for. He didn't need anyone's catty comments. Thank you Vinnie.

This same week in the popular room I tried to fit in with a group of girls. They were regulars and we were familiar with each other's style of type. One had quickly written something about a tent of which I interacted with. I thought the gesture was harmlessly friendly and we would find common ground to join together in some fun. Perhaps they would even share their ideas of entertainment but it was not to be. The girl was obviously whispered from the background by her friend and suddenly the girl typed in the room "Bertha burns the tent." Guess they childishly swear by cooties or something.

This particular summer I went online for the last time in the popular room by myself. Steve's nickname suddenly popped on the screen. I hadn't seen him in ages. "Hi, Steve"

"Get naked."

"After you." And then I tried ignoring him while communicating with the operators and nicer people.

"Perhaps the lady wants to show her stuff?"

"Let's take it into whisper Steve."

"No, in the room."

Oh gee, he was in a mood. I quickly whispered a male operator that this guy was trouble and to please watch. He acknowledged my request and I trusted that he would provide support.

Steve typed, "Work your magic."

Again I warned Steve in whisper that I was not comfortable flirting with him in the open forum. Again he stated where everyone could see, "In the room."

Oh, he was setting me up big time and I needed to play this in a very cool manner. The popular people knew that Ray and I were an item and would not be afraid to bring it to everyone's attention. But Steve was my fascination and of course I wanted to play with him even if the setting scenario was very uncomfortable. I know leaving then and there would have been the proper thing to do, but if I could just get Steve to say something overly sexual or derogatory the operator would be able to ban him from the room.

I started the game. "Lisa sits on Steve's lap and hugs him." I was nervous and knew people were watching but so far this was only simple flirtation.

"Where are my hands?" He asked.

"Where would you like them to be?"

"You tell me. Lady's preference."

I needed to be very careful so that my words didn't get too sexual. People would complain and request that we go into whisper. "Around my waist."

"Not on your thigh?"

One of the regular girls piped up and said something specifically to Steve and he in turn responded to her in a sexual manner. I quickly whispered this girl behind the scenes and asked if she knew him. No she did not came the reply. I warned her that he was major trouble and to be careful. She backed off instantly perhaps thinking that I was jealous, well maybe just a little.

My mind was completely distracted and shot now. I couldn't think straight and just sat there watching the room scroll by. Steve was also quiet for a short time before starting up again.

"Not in the mood today?"

"Nope." I replied.

"Boring." The lines scrolled a little more. A few lines later he instigated, "Perhaps you need some motivation. Would you like a hand up your skirt?"

I wondered where the operator was, he said he would help, but I wouldn't bother the man again. In hindsight it is now obvious that I was sending out mixed signals. If Steve needed to be told to shut up he should have been properly told to cease, but that wasn't the case. I wanted to play. I liked his attention any cheap way I could get it. So, in the long run it's no wonder that the operator did not come forward since he most likely saw me as a player and left the situation alone.

This chat was embarrassing and if it got back to Ray . . . well, it wouldn't be pretty. When I failed to respond Steve left the chat room. I then stepped up and embarrassed myself one more time in the room or so it seems. Pretending to be talking with the particular male operator I stated, "Sorry, I tried to get him to say more but it didn't work." To date this specific male operator avoids me and must assume that I'm trouble. It does hurt my feels since he doesn't know the complete story and sees me as less than worthy. The whole scenario could have been avoided if I had just left the room at the appropriate moment.

So I left the chat room for the last time that summer. Who needs this ridiculous kind of crap? I deleted Steve's name from messenger and this time I also deleted his addresses from my contact list. There was no going back now. This was it. Besides, if I was going to be a rich lady someday and in the public eye my reputation as well as Ray's reputation needed to be decent. The future was swiftly catching up with me. It was time to cover my tracks and clean up this dirty act that had been going on for three years.

But before straightening up my stupidity there was one more thing to do though. The next day I wished to rub salt into Steve's wounds. Without messenger there was little chance though, except to go into the chat site, call up his nickname and send an email through the service. The nasty email read as follows (the actual email):

> *Dear, Steve, Perhaps you should be let up to date with what's happening in the chat room. Word is buzzing around that other girls have informed operators that your nickname is a problem. Be careful. If the ops see you stirring the cauldron in the room you could be banned. Plus they have your IP (internet protocol) number and can ban for life. Yes I have also informed two ops of tension. Please don't try to cyber in the room. It's not accepted. Chat is chat, not to be taken seriously, and I don't. You intrigued me in the beginning to the point of obsession but it's mostly worn off. I know you disapprove that I have lied and cheated. Walk a mile in my shoes. And you have trouble with women. It shows. Perhaps you have been burned. Maybe they take advantage of the good side of your nature. I'm sure your career gets in the way too. I will always wonder what you look like and sound like but life goes on. Enjoy it Steve as we all deserve the best with what we make of it. Oh and I received the sports car. It's a blast!*

I actually did inform two operators of Steve's inappropriate behavior that afternoon of which they responded favorably to my request. Also I emailed the room owner over our inability to get along as well as his sadistic disposition and seven nicknames. She wrote a concise thank you note in return stating she would keep an eye out for his nicknames and also document the problem. Since that time I believe Steve has returned the favor. After sending him a portion of this manuscript he has since entered the room along with the room owner one morning. Thankfully Vinnie, Ray and I were on a roll discussing business and rides in exotic cars. Ray subsequently made a remark toward the 'pussy assed' lawyer and Steve's name instantly left the screen.

Later that afternoon after deleting Steve as a contact I checked the chat site but did not go into the room, none of man's nicknames were around but there was a nick titled 'L bite me'. It was also new on that specific day. Sure, I'll bite. What size chunk shall I take out? *LOL* Oh how I hope that it was him. If so it would mean that I had aroused his dander and then I win! And my men certainly know how challenge and winning are the most important things in the world to me. I won! We were finished and done and it felt good. Damn good. (Of course he was not totally gone, he would return in a surprising way.)

July 15th was almost here while licensing of the new security software was mere days away from becoming reality. Plans were in place for the two men to meet that weekend to go over specifics of the new software company. Vinnie stated that he had friends on Park Avenue in New York City and planned on staying in their luxury condo for the long weekend. Ray's enthusiasm was off the charts as well as mine. The money that was about to come in was going to help so many people, all the people that had helped Ray over the past several years would receive some benefit. Well, it was going to help lots of people except for his ex-wife. The idea was tossed about that maybe he should even take custody of their youngest daughter so that the ex would not receive a single dime out of this matter. Ray relished the thought quite strongly. In his inflated excitement he even told one good friend from work about the gigantic news that was about to unfold. The man quite honestly begged for his own future 'just don't forget me'.

Ray and I dreamed together—of building a large cabin deep in the woods together with a deck for sunning, the cars, Saleen, BMW, Lamborghini, but he remembered to take it slow at first. Don't blow the money in the beginning. Live between your means. You need to pay bills. Take care of insurance and build financial securities for the future should the flow of money unexpectedly end.

Ray said, "I can't believe this is really happening. How many people can say that they found their career from talking on the internet? Man, I can't imagine a million dollars. I even told Vinnie that he didn't need to give me millions, just give me the $150,000 every year. That's all I need to live on."

Thank goodness Ray was playing this venture smart, he knew better than to get caught up in all of our dreams before the money came through.

Saturday morning came along and Ray called me. I asked, "Have you talked to him yet?"

"Nope," he said with his voice falling off. Vinnie should have already been in contact with Ray.

"Maybe he found some hot chick on Park Avenue and got side tracked."

"Yeah," Ray replied barely hearing my joke.

The first road block was painful. Hours went past. Sunday arrived without a word from Vinnie. Ray hurt like hell but internalized the pain while I felt his ache but was helpless to be of any assistance. He desperately needed that sign on bonus to get on with life, to get into that new apartment real soon. Four weeks were now left to get out of the cabin and Ray sat vulnerable without a plan for the next phase of his existence. Monday arrived and Vinnie finally stepped foot out of the woodwork. The wealthy man's father had suffered a heart attack and Vinnie was a mess. He loved his dad very much he stated over and over.

"But you could've called me," Ray stated. "Just let me know you weren't coming out to New York."

"I know but I was just so busy. With dad in the hospital I couldn't think of anything else."

Ray thought that was still a poor excuse and I agree. Even in the middle of confusion a businessman would not leave a client hanging. At least a quick call to say that the meeting is off or I will get back with you as soon as possible. Perhaps some people have different ways of operating. But wouldn't you imagine that to become obviously wealthy one would be able to cover all areas of interest politely? Sugar goes a long way. Contacts are important. Business people have secretaries, assistants, helpers that are hired to relay information to contacts, or possibly my dream world of corporate business is warped. I think not.

Within a week or two Vinnie was back in business mode although his dad was still recovering from the heart attack and remained a critical issue that needed constant care. And then again there was another excuse that popped out of the blue when talks turned to Vinnie's physical meeting with Ray. Suddenly the rains came. (They actually did. Chicago received a bombardment of rain.) The basement of Vinnie's new house flooded and he was unable to get away for the weekend again.

During all this time I was telling my mother, sister and husband about Vinnie and Ray's venture. All three spoke up without hesitation. "Vinnie is a phony. He's not going to come through. There is no business." My husband smirked at the audacity of men so shallow inside to fool others without a sense of remorse. I trusted his common sense over the situation knowing he was right. Mom was suddenly worried about my mortality again and I accidentally made my sister cry. I rattled off to her about this stupid community and if this software business was true I would be gone soon. My brother-in-law took me aside at that point and asked what the heck was going on. He knows quite a bit of this story too.

From Ray's point of view he was cautious. He knew this was all too good to be true but needed to hold onto the dream for the sake of badly needed funds, and just having Vinnie as a friend made exhilaration of financial talks provide him with hope. Somehow or someway maybe cash would float in his direction. Vinnie promised. He said financial backing was going to happen in the near future. Vinnie returned to the conference table over and over stating that we're back on track. Scotty is finished creating the software.

Excuse me I thought he said Kirk created the software. Scotty Kirk, Kirk Scotty? Were we in the land of Star Trek? Beam me aboard Vinnie's multimillion dollar space ship! Sorry but I had to say it folks.

Hopes were played like this for weeks, back and forth, off and on. The man's business partner suddenly died. Also his best buddy totaled a motorcycle on the freeway and went careening down the concrete, removing a large percentage of his flesh. Doctors didn't know if the man was going to live or die. Vinnie was emotionally shot again while living in the hospital beside his friend. Excuses were constantly made and then quickly righted by the self described businessman including the fact that we suddenly found out he had cancer and needed surgery. Half of the time when Vinnie said he was on the phone he now stated that he was actually throwing up from chemo treatments. However concerning the surgery we never did figure out whether he actually had it or not because he was online most everyday chatting with his women.

One day he suddenly showed us a website for this new cancer technology that boosted the immune system by oxygenated white blood cells. Of course Vinnie was receiving these expensive innovated treatments. They seemed to be helping and he felt more energy than he had in a long time. The man praised the Lord for blessings in abundance.

Vinnie is a fast talker and relays more information than a person can take in. Day in and day out one could only listen to Ray's excitement as information came in over how the company would be run, how financial aspects of the company broke down into pieces of the corporate pie. I never actually understood processes completely but it didn't matter. As long as the men understood importance of managerial breakdown that was the main significance. They seemed to enjoy sharing these types of words with one another, discussing big business and dreaming as far as their minds could take esoteric matters.

September finally came. Ray had gotten extremely lucky with the cabin and received a much needed extension until the end of the month. This was it. Scotty Kirk had now actually finished creating the software and was going to meet with the two men on Monday. Ray felt that deadlines were finally being met and everything was going to inexhaustibly fall into place. I also felt my future really becoming reality. Vinnie had airline tickets. He was flying to Newburgh, New York on Friday afternoon to meet with Ray over dinner at a local restaurant. Ray, for protection in his own right, had also hounded Vinnie for the particular flight number and actually got it!

Friday evening came and went. I waited for the phone call to hear Vinnie's voice in the background, knowing with certainty the two men were laughing and having a great time. The phone call came late. That's alright I told myself as they were too busy to have called earlier but Ray's voice was not upbeat.

"Vinnie didn't show." He told me.

"I'm so sorry." I replied. "Maybe he'll show up tomorrow. Is Kirk still scheduled for Monday?"

"I don't think it's going to happen."

"You don't know." Reassurance was freely offered. I don't know why I continued playing the game when things seemed so hopeless. How much bull crap did we need spelled out? Where was the girl that verbally wrestled Steve while believing very little and living life as the biggest skeptic on this inflated round earth? We failed to see Vinnie online that weekend of course. In fact it was the following week before Ray even got word with the latest and greatest excuse. Vinnie had supposedly had a treatment that morning to oxygenate the white blood cells and then missed his flight. Kirk was also mad now that Vinnie could not get the project off the ground in a reasonable amount of time. Excuses continued as Vinnie was being pressured, to his frustration, by everyone in his business circle as well as purportedly pressuring his lawyers to finish contracts that had been stalled for months.

But sadly Ray reached his dreaded deadline. He needed to move out of the cabin within less than a week and barely had the damage deposit for an apartment. He informed Vinnie of this critical dilemma in hopes that the man could provide a last minute miracle of some sort.

"Here, let me send you $3,000 of the sign on bonus. This will tie you over and we'll work out everything later." The businessman generously offered.

The money failed to materialize that weekend of course. Ray's nerves were frayed from this stupidity but he stayed upbeat. "Don't worry about me I'll be just fine. I'll find something." Ray did continue to look at small apartments while considering each one carefully. I couldn't help my boyfriend financially and he knew this as well. There was no pressure from him for me to provide needed assistance. My husband was also aware of the constricting dilemma but did not bother to come forward either. It's not our responsibility although I care about the man tremendously. My husband and I can not support him financially. It is only realistic.

The next weekend Vinnie came out of the woodwork one more time with promises of the $3,000 sign on bonus meant to be delivered by Friday. Nothing happened. Saturday afternoon Ray checked Western Union again and also checked validity of the reference number. Nothing. Saturday night came and I received an uncharacteristic email from Ray stating that he was not in the mood to talk and that he was just going to go to bed.

That was not like Ray! He had reached the end of the road, the end of his limits. I slowly boiled to a simmer over the audacity of the rude businessman, the blatant phony. I tried calling my boyfriend but the ringer had been turned off so I quickly sent him an email stating my deep concern. Over time I had been telling Ray that if I ever got the chance to tell Vinnie to stick his promises where the sun doesn't shine I would without a doubt put Vinnie in his place. Ray continually stated just hold on and wait to see if something might materialize. Obviously something was never going to materialize! Ray was desperate and needed to hold onto a vision that was never going to happen and Vinnie needed someone to toy with, someone that idealized his prowess as an alleged powerful man. Well, I failed to see power from this shallow man and . . . the reader knows me by now. Vinnie's email address was in my possession.

> *Dear Vinnie, how can you hurt and demean another like this? Ray has given up hope on everything and it's all your fault. He's left at home tonight in tears because you never intended on sending the money in the first place. You didn't tell the truth and I see your short coming as deficient, especially for a businessman of your stature and ability.*
>
> *Don't you realize that he has to be out of the cabin in a few days and needs that money desperately? What you are doing to the man is criminal and I don't feel one bit bad about bringing this to your attention. Have a good day, Lisa*

How did I think I could get by with talking to Vinnie this way? What did it matter? What he was doing to Ray was sick, mental abuse. So by early morning I received a little email letter and it went very close to this:

> *Dear Lisa, I don't see where this is any of your fucking business. The talks between Ray and I are in reference to my company which you have nothing to*

*do with. Plus I don't see where you have the right to talk to your boyfriend's future employer in this tone. If Ray is in need of a mommy figure such as you then I don't see where he has any business being CEO of such a large company. I need to stop and question his ability to run my business. And by the way, people that live in glass houses should not throw stones. What would your husband think of all this? Does he know that you are fucking Ray? Maybe you should just remain a mommy figure to him and leave Ray and me to our talks. Have a good day.*

My laughter was extremely hardy. Oh this was fun! Mmm, Aries men, they do like the challenge of a battle but so do I. Taking a deep cleansing breath I gathered my wits and analyzed the main content of the letter, along with his words complete with all the mistakes and misspellings.

*Dear Vinnie, cute, very cute the way you lose control of your emotions and foolishly lash out at the world. Ray is a very strong man and you know it. You've said so your self that he has a good head for business. It is you that has failed him. He needed your assistance in the worst way possible. He needed that down payment on an apartment really bad and you failed to be there for him. Oh, and by the way, my house is not glass. My husband is completely aware that I have a boyfriend and allows me the luxury. Do not speak of things you know nothing of Vinnie. It's not a good practice. You never intended on giving Ray the money. Prove me wrong. Lisa*

Man! I didn't know I had this fortitude inside. Honestly I was shaking in my shoes because he did sound legitimate in communication but he couldn't have been the person he portrayed. Not with all the outrageous excuses and poor choices in projecting the image of a professional. Frankly he had failed to provide Ray with professionalism at its best.

Vinnie was on the ball this morning of our brutal attacks and there was yet another letter.

*Dear Lisa, you are completely out of line. After reviewing matters with my business partner we have decided that Ray is not the man for the job. You have just lost him the position. I hope you're proud of yourself now. We do not feel that Ray is stable enough to run a company of this magnitude and therefore we resign his request for the position. About the money, my brother sent it this morning but since receiving your email we have now cancelled the order. It would be a good idea if you back down and reevaluated yourself Lisa. What do you think Ray would say to all this? I don't think he would be very happy with your attitude. Prove me wrong. Vinnie*

Laughter ensued again after reading the letter. The man certainly was full of himself however I was not done.

*Dear Vinnie, Ray never had the position because it never existed. You and your partner didn't just decide this fact because you've been leading Ray on for months now. You are quite a character. Besides, I thought your partner was dead. I'm turning my computer off now and going for a power run. Have a good day, Lisa*

I did turn off the computer and walk away, put my sneakers on and prepared to go outside. But something told me to turn the computer back on one more time. There was one more email from Vinnie.

*Dear Lisa, a power run? Isn't a power trip enough for you? This useless drivel is a waste of my time. I'm barring your nickname from my email address. Have a good life with Ray.*

I turned off the computer and walked away preparing to enjoy my walk on this sunny day only to have the phone ring. It was Ray.

"What's going on?"

"What do you mean?"

"I just got a series of emails from Vinnie. Seems the two of you have been having strong words this morning."

Oh crap, the gig was up. I was caught and hoped that I had not written anything too outrageous to cause embarrassment. Ray knew my zest for living. He was accepting of the mere fact. "He sent you the emails?" I cautiously inquired.

"Yes. I'm reading them now." He stated.

Quickly speaking in total defense, "You were upset last night and I couldn't let him get by with this stuff anymore."

"I thought you told me you weren't going to say anything to him just yet."

"Last night was the last straw," my statement was made in all honesty for protection because Ray didn't sound too happy with the unfolding situation.

He read a little more. "Wow, you two were brutal."

"Hell yeah, he can't get by with this crap."

"You just couldn't keep your mouth shut could you? It's that damn need for challenge." Ray paused for a moment as he thought. "I've got a plan and I want you to play along with me. You need to write an email to him and apologize."

"What?! Apologize to him! You've got to be kidding. I'm not apologizing to him. He's a creep that's been leading you on."

"Just listen to me. I want you to create an email. You can do this. Tell him that you've just gotten off the phone with me. We had a fight. I was very upset with you for loosing my job and now we're breaking up."

"I can't do that."

"Yes you can, put your acting skills to work." He heard me sigh. "Tell him that we had words and that I chewed you out really bad. Of course we're not really breaking up but pretend like you've been crying."

"This is crazy."

"Pour it on thick so he believes us."

"Why bother?" I asked with thick sarcasm.

"Because I don't want to fight with anybody, I don't like it when my friends fight."

"Ray, he's not worth it, he's a liar and a phony. He's only been leading you on. He's not a real businessman." At that moment if I had been paying any attention at all I would have noticed that Ray was still considering Vinnie to be a friend even after this stupidity. My common sense is telling me one thing and my heart is telling me another. Thankfully my strong independence is still firmly in place unable to be penetrated by anything I deem inappropriate.

Ray continued reprimanding, "You haven't been talking to him, you don't understand. It really is none of your business. Just write this email for me, alright?"

"But he's deleted me from his address. My addy is blocked."

"Then use Connie's email address." Ray was referring to the address that I used to fool Steve while portraying the businesswoman.

This was beyond crazy. Apologize to that creep? Ray was my boyfriend that I cared for deeply. Of course we weren't really breaking up. I would support and back him with strong vengeance to the ends of the earth. So, with a deep sigh at the time, I supposed that this phony apology could be created except for one mere fact . . . Vinnie would not believe regret from this vindictive woman one bit. What did I care? As long as Ray was happy with my compliance to his wishes what the hell. My acting skills were severely on the line.

*Dear Vinnie, I can't believe this is happening. Ray called and now we're through. You wouldn't believe the things that he said to me. I apologize for hurting your feelings. Excuse me while I dry my eyes. I'm still in shock. Ray said some really awful things to me. I didn't want this to happen because I still love him very much. But he is through with our relationship now.*

---

*Perhaps you have words of wisdom for someone that is going through the pain of a breakup. Sorry to bother you, Lisa*

It would take a real idiot to believe those words I imagined. A few days later Vinnie called Ray apologizing profusely while stating he did not mean to cause us to break up. Vinnie, the hopeless romantic, instructed Ray to tell me that he wasn't mad and hoped to see us online again soon. *Shaking my head here and listening to the rattling of loose screws deep inside.*

The super hero continues telling Ray to this day, "Please inform Lisa that I'm not angry."

Excuse me for one moment, but does a woman's voice matter? I see a crime to humanity needs to be addressed here, but alas it seems that inhumane crimes matter very little to some, the perpetrator or the victim. Why should I bother continuing with any of this mess?

Alright, this ridiculous fiasco has to create a point to some degree. Vinnie must have admitted to himself that he had been playing Ray all along and that his conscience rose enough to prove malicious deflections of reality. Or as Ray tells me a lie is simply a lie, there is no deflection.

Three months after this dramatic episode Vinnie did admit to Ray that the software company never came to completion which only proves that Vinnie did lie several times, or as Vinnie says business was stalled unable to get off the ground. The current status of the software company is shelved for now since there is a problem with the government's acceptance of it. The problem is legitimate and understandable, but still. It is amazing how some projects materialize without so much as a glitch, and then there are some that get stuck in the muck of legalities, unable to come to fruition within a reasonable amount of time. After a large amount of time if the project cannot come forward it either needs a serious shot in arm or else dropped like a hot potato. With any luck you would imagine that a good businessman could inject that shot in the arm knowing who and how to push to get the ball rolling once again. But in this case it is the government—and that word in itself says slower than a seven year itch. Obviously, so who has the correct answer now?

Vinnie and Ray are still friends to this day and talk on the phone once in awhile. It is absolutely none of my business. Vinnie continues to rattle off huge stories while stating probability of a position for his friend someday. He persists in dangling the carrot in front of Ray's nose which my boyfriend needs badly. In my biased opinion it's just not fair.

I would also like to interject that a verbal crime was also made at one point in their exchange, but since it is none of my business however the crime cannot be told. Does the emotional health and lively hood of one person matter? Oh course it does, and if one tells another to give up an extremely important portion of their life for a reward that does not come worth, well, a crime capable of being adjusted in the criminal justice system is worthy of being brought to light. The reward or crime was later recanted in typical format by excess of excuses. It is a good thing that my boyfriend did not give up that extremely important portion of his life. We are not talking about giving up family or friendship's here either. In all actuality this paragraph has little meaning because who am I to argue a cause for anyone? Sarcasm remains supreme.

Also Vinnie's overly dramatic health stories continue with little crises. It seems that there are some people in this world that do suffer continuing adverse health conditions, very sad stories indeed but somehow this man's conditions seem, well, just too far fetched—over and over again, monthly or weekly. It's beyond hypochondriac. One must boldly assume that adverse health conditions would greatly affect one's ability to do actual physical labor or subsequently hinder one's weekly budding romances. I must also question why someone would bother sharing all this drama with another man when it is private misery, but then again I wrote this diary. Frustration without the reward of conclusion is also supreme.

So where did this super hero come from? And why? We may never know but his game of deception is down pat. We never heard the man ask for money since he only makes offer of it. In summation this person's only basic crime seems to be of wanting, needing attention, to be admired for his prowess as a fantastic businessman. Perhaps he was once capable of great things but it would seem that his edge has been filed down to the dull point of no return. I think our hero is a has-been, physically as well as mentally, unless he can actually prove otherwise. These words are not issued as a challenge but only as curiosity searching for the blatant truth. Of course this is all my biased opinion and does not matter to some since it is none of my business to begin with, however Ray's wellness is certainly my concern.

This episode did affect us on a large scale and it took several weeks to recover my bearings from the ridiculous fiasco. I didn't realize how much the idea of wealth had affected me. Dreams of the glamorous future had motivated and changed the very course of my life. While completely giving up on this community I was seriously ready to walk away and start that new life with freedom and emotional support beside Ray. In three months, six months, no more than a year I would be out of here. Rejoicing deep inside while knowing freedom was directly around the corner I hoped and dreamed of a new existence in a different place. It was all because of Ray that my life was evolving in this new direction. Then the door suddenly slammed in my face that fateful day. It hurt, hurt really bad. One can only imagine the harsh pain that Ray actually endured, of the rich carrot dangling with exuberant reward and then suddenly disappearing.

Excitement of the future came and went in a climatic moment of ruthless, vibrant banter. The lush happiness that flashed before our eyes failed to materialize while reality hammered down hard proving that I am going nowhere. I never was. This boring little town in the Midwest is my home, my pets need me, and my husband needs me, my family, mom and sister. How do they put up with my crazy antics?

As I buckle down to daily living while trying to give my home its full attention Ray still keeps calling every day, sometimes twice a day or three times. This leaves me torn to no end. I need to be true to myself, my family and this house but I also care about Ray. He needs me. He needs to be loved and accepted without pretence but this friendship is draining me. I would be happy with one phone call every other day and eventually tapering to once a week but Ray won't hear of it. I have told him. I have tried.

Never has a man controlled me, well, as a typical daughter, not since my father. Ray has control over me and he knows it. He humorously calls it 'making me feel guilty' for not letting him get his way. Oh, believe me this woman gets her way often, but maybe an outsider would question how much control Ray really does have over our relationship or how much control I allow him to have. He calls it our love for one another. Do I truly have the ability to actually love another? Well, that sounds like another chapter of which I won't touch with a ten foot pole.

*Turning up the CD while blaring Van Halen's 'Running with the Devil' and walking away from this blasted computer.*

Perhaps just sticking our head into the sand will get us through this stupid medium called life.

# CONCLUSION

So in conclusion I have faced myself—battled forward with sword in hand against demons which hindered the growth of a worthwhile soul. Confrontation has been made of the lingering darkness that resides within the very core of many of us. My internal rage has greatly softened now as is the need to revolt against . . . brick walls that hold me in or obsession over ridiculous matters.

The need to argue with the big boys is over for now anyway. I've managed to hold my own against two wealthy and powerful Aries and one bull headed Taurus. But what good has it really done? Where has it gotten me? There is no satisfaction to this useless quest. They continue to hold their opinions, opinions that are only decisive theories of one another, and a theory is not a complete profile of any actual individual. Or in my husband's case we agree to just live with it and stay married. I've proven very little through these heated battles except that perhaps I am quite capable of being a bully too.

We are all only human. Each individual is given this basic persona to mold, grow, cherish and share with others. We do the best with what we have to work with, of knowledge that each of us has gained through childhood, the turbulent teen years and trials of adulthood. Well, most of us do the best we can. Some could and should try a little harder. But alas, we are not all perfectionists beating our heads against a brick wall trying to force objects that will not budge and it's simply alright. This vast world takes all kinds. It has and always will. Thank goodness for our special differences. What a boring world this would be if people were all the same.

Chat rooms have finally lost their appeal thanks to Vinnie for destroying our dreams of a comfortable future and for Steve wishing to humiliate me in the room. Steve has since proven we can now be in the same space without tarnishing each others reputation.

I do go online when boredom easily sets in but chat rooms are nothing less than trouble, nonsense and drama, and seriously who needs all that bull? I still communicate in instant messenger at least once or twice a week, except sitting at the computer on a constant basis (clinically known as a mouse potato) does get rather boring.

My men are still with me, husband and Ray. Nemesis Steve's nickname sits quietly in messenger and Brad resides in messenger as well.

One particular day while doing research on a certain kind of software a strange thing happened. There was suddenly a voice clip of man with the same name as Brad. Quite excited I listened. It was him! Along with his complete name, title and company name. He is the CEO—the executive officer of the company. This was an exceptional find. I knew Brad was an important man but little did I know how important. I traced the company's leads and researched their position in the market, their staff and product. One could only be impressed by grandeur. It stated their funding, who formed the company and their clientele. Brad is a big dog in this world. Just the way I like it. I wouldn't have it any other way. Mmm, powerful men, men influential enough to move mountains if so inclined. Damn. This little girl just feels fortunate enough to have held short interview with a man such as this.

My research did not stop there as I continued prompting sites. Within a matter of moments there was another site that flattered their company's makeup. Suddenly I heard another voice clip and moved the curser over. This time there was a video of Brad and he was talking in the video. I stared at the computer as my mouth dropped open with a smile bursting across my face. There was Brad and he was not young like the photo he had given me. The photo of the young man with peaches and cream complexion and blonde hair with blue eyes had been around for possibly 25 years. But I continued to stare in amazement. He had claimed to be six years younger than me but reality was proving that he was more likely four to six years older. It didn't matter. Brad was still a handsome man, quite confident, polished and fearless in manner. And I enjoyed watching him talk with his hands. Umm, wonder what those roaming hands could do for me?

I waited a couple of weeks before telling him that I had found out his identity. He deserved to know this truth. But before exposing the new found secret there was temptation to stretch it out and tease a little more. I teased him about business meetings which he seems to juggle on a regular basis. "Tell your boss," I stated, "that you want to run the show for a change." He laughed. Another time I stated, "Tell your boss I want to conduct the meeting today."

He replied with a laugh, "You're funny. I like your energy."

It was on a Saturday morning that I revealed the secret. It was best that he learn about this serious matter within the comforts of home. Thank goodness the man was not too stunned nor completely surprised about the revelation perhaps because he is high profile. I assured him that strict confidence was firmly in place. We would never reveal or cause complication to one another and he replied that I am a special lady. This man also has documentation of my home phone number and is well aware of my full name and of where I can be found, but he will not go that route. I am completely confident.

All this is fine and dandy but what Brad and I have done can be viewed as being completely inappropriate in family instances. It certainly could have been labeled an emotional affair but it never actually became that evolved. Well, maybe at times it seemed to be that evolved. He and I do not chat every week and sometimes go months at a time between communications but we have known each other for a few years now. It must also be said that we no longer have phone sex due to circumstances, only flirtatious instant messages.

What Brad has done online is an addiction as is my addiction as well. Any form of sexual addiction is wrong and harmful to our loved ones. It robs our loved ones of attention that needs to be directed only toward them, directed at the vows that we made before God and family. I know this, understand this and so does Brad. Therefore although we acknowledge our fun we manage to keep the compulsion under control.

So what does this say about my physical affair with Ray? I know and accept all consequences.

Steve . . . he knows better than to take chat seriously. One day I opened my alter ego's email, Connie, only in attempt to keep the address active but suddenly saw Steve online in instant messenger. He was also well aware that I came online. My real name was listed at the time and I quickly changed it to Connie's name to avoid confrontation, as if that would make any difference. How in the world did I forget to delete Steve's nickname from Connie's contacts? It was too late.

"Hi." He said.

"Hello."

"Who is this?" Steve played.

"Connie, the businesswoman from the Midwest. We chatted a long time ago."

"Did we have fun?"

"Yes." I answered. Wow, Steve had just graciously opened the door for us to start off with a new footing. We tried being polite to one another, not chatting for long periods of time because condescension begins rearing its ugly head. This next chance didn't last long either. Our nicknames still sit in instant messenger but of course it seems we are on non-speaking terms right now.

One must give the man credit that he is highly intelligent. I will always be curious as to who the man is behind the dark mask that engaged my fascination. Remember, he gave the persona of the ideal American male. He says that he is not handsome. Looks can only go so far my rapid reply volley's in return. What resides within all of us is what matters, knowledge, adeptness, caring and compassion. At this point the lawyer would tell me that compassion comes from my husband.

Unless you understand whether my husband knows how to implement compassion or not don't bother trying to counsel me, Steve. Save that for your clients.

Alas, our conversations have fallen to the wayside. There is very little substance left to banter with. So why does he still hang around? Or does he still hang around? I'm not so certain anymore. Perhaps my soul used to fascinate him almost as much as his soul fascinates me, or sadly, maybe it's best to keep an enemy at arms length at all times. He would tell me this is completely bull shit and then say 'bye'. 'Whatever' to coin a word that he uses so well. It would have been nice to get back to the days when our conversations were fun, frivolous and not threatening.

Should any reader believe in reincarnation perhaps this antagonistic association could be put into different terms. Steve and I have most likely crossed paths once before . . . say medieval times. A very cruel landlord put an end to my life as I adamantly defended my husband's opinion based on heated issues of the day. (Do I still not defend men's opinions over heated issues?) Physically removed from our home I was taken away from my family in a fitful sight of kicking and screaming. My life ended quietly and alone while imprisoned in the small room of a stone monstrosity. (Am I still locked up within four confining walls? Is this my cross to bear in life?) Of course Steve would have been that landlord or Duke that had locked me away in an effort to shut me up.

But those times are no more. Steve is unable to touch me in this lifetime. There is no longer reason to dislike the man or take his negative pushiness seriously. I look at it this way—the life of a lawyer cannot be easy. Although they claim to not become emotionally attached to their cases, one can only assume that some cases do weigh heavily on their minds. No wonder he drinks premium vodka. He also seems to always be reading and states that he gets sleepy eyes at the end of the day. The man works very hard and chat is only a small momentary release from daily pressures. I know I should not give an inch to his sadistic mentality but I do. His life is his own and a contradiction to mine.

Near the end of this line of men resides the best. Ray continues to state, "You never meant to fall in love." Nope, not in my wildest dreams my dear man. I will be concerned about your welfare and love you until the end of time. Ray is my equal. On a mental and emotional level we reside at the same temporal point. In a different life I am certain we could mesh together with a worthwhile existence.

Falling into my thoughts, should I ever feel guilty about my affair with Ray . . . well, I don't feel guilty. It is sweet desire that is much deserved. I deserve to accompany a man that is capable of displaying a well rounded personality, a real man that can look after a woman, give her support and nurture her best qualities. Then why do I allow thoughts of Steve to still cloud my emotion? Perhaps it's not what the all American boy could offer after all but only the fact that I will never have the perfection that I'm searching or wishing for. Even with this fact, Ray is still hopeful that one day his future will become brighter and he will be able to offer that grand existence.

My sister and mother continue to discourage me from association with Ray. They like Ray as a person and as a friend but just don't want to see me get hurt. My husband realizes I have a lifelong relationship with the man and graciously accepts the fact. What am I going to do about it? Times are changing quickly now. Ray has now moved out of the cabin to an apartment closer to work near the Hudson River. Happily he is doing well and has a roommate to split expense with. Each week reveals more. We shall see. Ray has no intension of taking me away from my husband right now and claims he can share me for many years to come. "Take things slowly, one day at time. No one knows what the future will bring." He says.

These past three years have drawn us closer than ever. Ray tells me that I am afraid to admit certain truths and he is quite possibly right. I am fearful of the future, fearful of disrupting a routine of which I've become accustomed to, fearful of needlessly hurting anyone as well. However Ray states that he loves me even more. And because he feels this way it scares me knowing we can't have what we want. Again he would say, "You never meant to fall in love."

When Ray first came along I was attention starved. That goes without saying. Steve and Brad had certainly seen the undertones of starvation. Brad and I discussed lack of attention from our marriage partners when he stated that I make him feel alive again. Those are wonderful words to hear from someone, very flattering. And then Steve read right through me besides the fact that I told him way too much about my personal life, personal things of which he never fully understood. His excuse for chatting—there was never enough. Meaning there was never enough female attention smothered over his ego, besides never enough sexy photos from women for him to view. I quickly obliged giving him everything I could, and Brad too for that matter but on a different level. Unfortunately it was all a game—for all three of us even though I tried to make more out of it.

And then Ray came along while I still suffered from slow lingering neglect from a marriage that was barely there. I fell in love with this guy but only treated him like another nickname. Steve and Brad had been so engraved into my brain that it took a long time to wean away from them. With many months, even years behind us I've finally become able to concentrate on the one that I truly fell in love with, Ray. Although I didn't burn bridges with Steve and Brad completely, I kept the other two around but not at the same stage as before because Ray and I were becoming closer and closer each day.

So now we're to a point where we are happy, happy but frightened at the same time with what we have. We've propelled to a new plateau. Falling in love with Ray was not supposed to happen but it did. Another scary thing is I didn't know that love could be like this nor did I expect to find it this way either.

To philosophize again—perhaps it's not always about a persons needs and wants. Life is about how one feels inside. Are you happy? Are you content with your being and space where your feet continue to tread upon the ground?

Contemplate this—if you were alone while stranded on an island your anxious existence would be all consumed over your needs and wants, or merely survival in its most basic form such as finding food and building shelter. The human communication factor is nonexistent while your fearful emotions take over. There are no outside influences to direct a path. Your instincts are your own and the choices you make decide the extent of success. But alas here in the midst of complicated civilization we plod along in this emotional daily grind doing the best that we can, brushing past a multitude of souls journeying in the same direction. Our choices overlap and merge in communal assistance. Put a smile on your face as you plod along, stroll or dance an Irish jig. Rise above the mediocre. Don't forget to say please and thank you for it's the positive image that we project to one another through this daily grind. Life is to be lived, lived to the fullest and propelled from the heart.

While surmising basic human nature the comment must also be made that 'dream men' do not exist just as the 'Barbie doll' or 'Miss America' does not exist for men. Perfect men only exist in our dreams or in how far your imagination can take you. Pity that our world is not a perpetual fairytale. Wouldn't that leave me in perpetual heaven?

Men can be obliging and open doors, flatter us, admire us, provide remarkable romance and sensuality, but not all men can be all things at all times. Forget about teaching men new tricks. Wrong. Wrong. Wrong. Not unless women are willing to learn new tricks as well. Share and learn together. Spend quality time together. Communication is the positive key in getting along with the person beside you as Ray has taught me well. Look your significant other in the eye and ask him/her what is on their mind, listen and care. During this process merge your thoughts with theirs in complete understanding. The progressive result can rekindle lost considerations.

As I end this book it's with a sense of sadness. Not for a sense of loss but with a sense of closure, closure of the past. The first forty some odd years are finished and behind me. My husband and I are still trying. We now have a cruising motorcycle which helps our togetherness, along with the fun loving pact we run with most every Sunday if the weather is right.

Some days I still fall into the trap of disliking this community and yearn for something new with a little more support but sadly the daily grind continues. Our family and friends still see us as the lucky ones living a content life free from the heavy restraint of responsibility. No one knows what the future will bring or should it bring anything outstanding at all. I will continue watching the nieces and nephews grow and will help my favorite eccentric Irish teen through this crazy thing called life.

Well, I received the sexy little sports car and it is very sweet. Some days I leave the house with those designer sunglasses and an ego over inflated with confidence and those good fitting jeans. Sure I'm almost 50. Does it look like I care? I have been accused of being on a power trip by Vinnie from Chicago that soars on his own self imposed power trip. A trip is the only place where I have control. It's the only place that matters.

Driving the sports car 85 mph while quickly glancing around for traffic the coast is clear on the freeway. Tower to pilot 'you're free to fly'. Pressing the accelerator the engine accepts its mission and we instantly propel to 100 mph. The solid block and suspension hold tight. There is no shimmy, no vibration as the intricate engine purrs like a kitten and begs for more. Your wish is my command . . . sharply pressing the accelerator to the floor while blowing the windscreen off the last page. Now that's power baby!

www.ingramcontent.com/pod-product-compliance
Lightning Source LLC
Chambersburg PA
CBHW031548080326
40690CB00054B/738